Sue
2013

♡

Good one !

How to Make Upside-down Dolls

ALSO BY JOHN COYNE

The Penland School of Crafts Book of Jewelry Making
The Penland School of Crafts Book of Pottery
By Hand: A Guide to Schools and a Career in Crafts

How to Make Upside-down Dolls

by JOHN COYNE
and JERRY MILLER

BOBBS-MERRILL

INDIANAPOLIS / NEW YORK

Published by the Bobbs-Merrill Company, Inc.
Indianapolis / New York

Library of Congress Cataloging in Publication Data

Coyne, John.
  How to make upside-down dolls.

  1. Dollmaking.   I. Miller, Jerry, 1946-   joint
  author.   II. Title.

TT175.C69   745.59'22   77-76889
ISBN 0-672-52157-1

Designed by Bernard Schleifer
Manufactured in the United States of America

FIRST PRINTING

To Jennifer and Patricia Coyne

Contents

Introduction

THE UPSIDE-DOWN DOLLS made by the women in the mountains of western North Carolina are as old as the hills themselves. "I can remember my grandmother making such dolls for me," explained one woman of the Crafts Unlimited cooperative, "and now I'm making them for my own grandchildren."

Often these dolls were the only toys that a child had. Families in these remote hills and hollows were too poor and too far away from cities to purchase manufactured toys. The dolls were created from scraps left over after mothers had made clothes for the family.

These dolls were often Christmas presents. "I can remember one time I got a Snow-White doll for Christmas," recalls another dollmaker. "It was the prettiest doll I ever did see. 'Course my mother had a real gift for upside-down dolls and she made them for all the other little girls in our parts."

The upside-down dolls made in North Carolina are unusual in that storybook characters are joined in one doll. This is the only area in America where one can find such combinations, and how it all came about no one knows.

The dolls were not made for a commercial market until the late 1960s when the Office of Economic Opportunity began to develop the indigenous hand crafts in these depressed areas as a way of providing a source of income for the women of the mountains. Although it costs these women only six dollars to make a doll, they are sold in craft shops in large cities like New York and Chicago for fifty dollars apiece.

It takes these mountain women only two or three hours to finish a doll. They use patterns that have been standardized by the cooperative and are the same ones found in this book. The women make the dolls in their homes, or when possible, they gather at the headquarters of Crafts Unlimited in Lenoir, North Carolina. The making of these dolls then becomes both a source of income and a chance to get together with neighbors.

Upside-down dolls are made by a number of craft cooperatives in the Appalachian Mountains, but the dolls made by the women of Crafts Unlimited are unique in that they are larger dolls and they are finished with a greater care for details.

All the dollmakers take a special interest in their creations, and every doll is signed by the maker. They are always curious to know where their dolls were sold and to whom. Often they will receive letters from little girls, thanking them for making the dolls.

This book is the first time any of these upside-down dolls have been shown in a "how-to" fashion. The patterns and instructions given were developed with the women of Crafts Unlimited. We thank them for their time and for showing us how to make these wonderful dolls.

John Coyne

One: *BEFORE YOU START*

Here are some hints and suggestions for making the dolls in this book. They will help you make beautiful and well-made upside-down dolls, dolls that will last a long, long time.

ALL ABOUT FABRICS

Corduroy: Doesn't ravel very much but you need to cut all parts in the same direction of the material.

Cotton: Use a cotton blend if possible. Cotton blends don't wrinkle and they wash. Also, they do much better than 100% cotton.

Plush fabrics: The pattern should be placed on the fabric in one direction so that the pile runs downward.

Felt: Can't be washed! Felt will also give if stuffed too tightly or pulled at a seam. If felt is used for the body of a doll, always line it with muslin. Pattern parts can be cut in any direction.

Muslin: It is very easy to use and sews well.

Sheath Lining: Will ravel easily and is difficult to sew as it slides. It helps to allow more seam allowance with this fabric.

Terry: Some grades (thicknesses) of terry cloth will pull apart when stuffed tightly. Make sure you have a thick, tightly woven piece of terry cloth.

ALL ABOUT CUTTING

Iron materials before cutting and sewing, especially if they are very wrinkled. Cut all materials with the grain. To be certain that the material is okay for cutting, make sure that the horizontal and vertical grains are in rectangular form. Fabrics with a nap (corduroy) should be cut with the nap running in one direction. One-directional prints should be cut like a nap fabric, but all-over prints with no definite design can be cut like a plain fabric. With plush fabrics, cut only the backing, not the pile.

Pattern pieces should be pinned on light materials like cotton, but on heavier materials it would be easier to draw the pattern with a tailor's chalk and then cut it. Since all cutting is done in the beginning, attach the pattern with a pin onto the fabric so you can find it easily and refer to it while working.

SEWING AND STITCHING

It's advisable to machine-stitch the dolls' heads and bodies, as they have to be stuffed. Clothes may be done by hand.

Set the machine for 12 stitches per inch for regular stitching. Set the machine for 5 stitches per inch for basting or gathering. Basting the material is not necessary, but it is very helpful, especially for someone new at making dolls. Sheath lining should always be basted before sewing. It would also help to baste the more complicated pieces before sewing. Seams should be pressed after sewing. Top-stitching can be done either by machine or by hand, depending on what is easier.

Here are the stitches most commonly used in making upside-down dolls.

Back Stitch: This is a small stitch used when top-stitching by machine would be too difficult. Work the stitch from right to left. Bring the needle up through the fabric to the right side. Insert it one or two fabric threads behind the place where the thread came out, and bring the needle forward and out ⅛″ (3 mm.) from the back stitch. Begin each additional stitch just outside the preceding stitch. (Fig. 1).

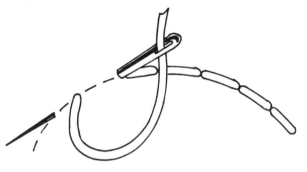

Fig 1: *Back stitch*

Slip Stitch: This stitch is used for hemming as well. Slip the needle in the fold. Bring the needle out of the fold and take up a thread of the other piece at the same point. Slip the needle through the material about ¼″ (6 mm.). Continue the stitch. (Fig. 2). When hemming, the stitch can be as long as ½″ (1.25 cm.).

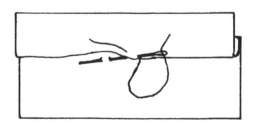

Fig. 2: *Slip stitch*

Whip Stitch: This stitch is used for hemming two pieces of fabric together. It is also used for sewing the dolls together, or the arms to the body, etcetera. Work the stitch from right to left. Bring the needle up through the edge of one piece and put the needle in the fabric over the edge of the other piece. Then bring the needle out through the first piece. (Fig. 3).

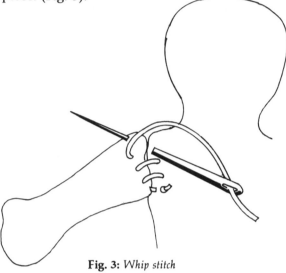

Fig. 3: *Whip stitch*

Hem Stitch: This is a perfect stitch for hemming, especially when the two pieces of fabric are uneven. Work the stitch from right to left. Bring the needle up through the hem edge. Take a stitch directly opposite and outside the hem, catching only one thread of the fabric; then direct the needle diagonally up through the hem edge. Space the stitches about ¼-⅜″ (6-9 mm.) apart. (Fig. 4).

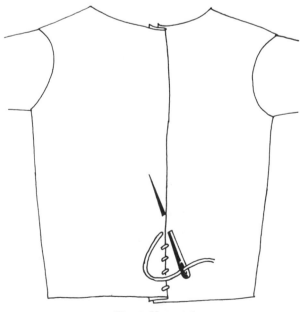

Fig. 4: *Hem stitch*

Buttonhole Stitch: Work this stitch from right to left. Start by bringing the thread to the left and then to the right to form a loop around the edge where the stitch will be made. Insert the needle from the underside up through the fabric, but keep the thread behind both the point and the eye of the needle. Hold the loop with the left thumb and pull the needle up through the fabric, then away from you to place the purl of the stitch on the edge of the fabric. (Fig. 5).

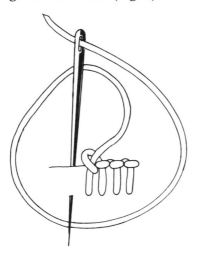

Fig. 5: *Buttonhole stitch*

French Knot: The French knot is an embroidery stitch. Knot the long end of the thread. Bring the needle up through the fabric at the point where the knot is to be made. Hold the needle close to the fabric and wind the thread two or three times around the point. Hold the thread taut around the needle and insert the needle through the fabric close to the point where the thread came out. (Fig. 6. Arrow in illustration indicates spot where needle is inserted after wrapping thread around needle.) Place the thumb over the knot to hold

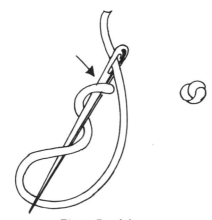

Fig. 6: *French knot*

the twist in place and pull the thread through to the underside, bringing the knot snugly against the fabric.

Outline Stitch: This stitch is used for embroidering eyes, eyebrows, etcetera. Work the stitch from left to right with the needle pointed to the left. Bring the needle up through the fabric from the underside. Make small back stitches, lapping each stitch slightly by bringing the needle out about $\frac{1}{16}$" (1.25 mm.) behind the previous stitch. (Fig. 7).

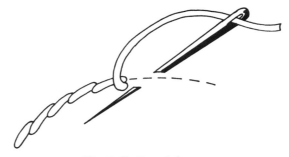

Fig. 7: *Outline stitch*

Straight Stitch: This stitch is used mainly for embroidering eyelashes, etcetera. Bring the needle up through the fabric at the start of an eyelash line. Then take the needle down through the fabric at the point where the eyelash line ends and bring it up again at the start of the next eyelash line. (Fig. 8).

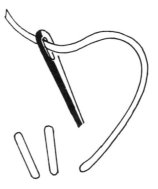

Fig. 8: *Straight stitch*

Lazy-Daisy Stitch: Bring the thread up in the center of the "flower." Hold the thread down with the thumb; insert the needle close to or in the exact spot where the thread emerged and bring it out the desired distance away. Now draw through over the working thread. Tie down with a tiny stitch made over loop as shown in illustration. (Fig. 9). Make similar stitches to form a circle around the same center point.

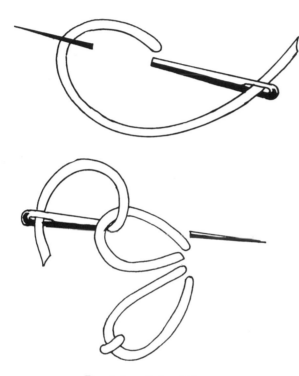

Fig. 9: *Lazy Daisy stitch*

Satin Stitch: Begin by bringing up the needle at one edge of the area to be covered. Insert the needle at the opposite edge and return to the starting line by carrying it underneath the fabric. Make the stitches close enough to cover background fabric completely. (Fig. 10).

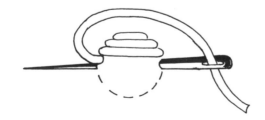

Fig. 10: *Satin stitch*

ALL ABOUT STUFFING

Polyester fiberfill is the best stuffing because it is flame resistant. Also, it can be washed. Stuff the arms first. Do not use anything sharp for the stuffing—it might cut through the fabric. The doll is correctly stuffed when it is "bouncy."

If the seam breaks while stuffing then begin over again and resew the seam. Once the stuffing is firm and the body of the doll is "bouncy," then stitch the opening closed.

WORKING TIPS

A place to work

Find a flat large surface to hold your work and give you a place to develop the patterns. You will also need the flat working space for cutting and later for keeping the cut materials and finished pieces.

SOME SEWING NICETIES

Your upside-down dolls will look lovelier if extra care is taken in finishing them. Make sure that the buttons match and that they are firmly stitched to the doll. Clip off any loose threads. Tie the ribbons neatly.

MATERIALS AND SUPPLIES

You will need

tape measure and six-inch ruler
tissue paper
dark pencil or felt pen
magic transparent tape
iron
scissors
thimble
blunt tool for stuffing
an assortment of threads, hand and machine needles, straight pins

ENLARGING PATTERNS

Most patterns are actual size and need only to be traced from the book. A few large pattern pieces are shown on a grid and must be enlarged to full size.

In these patterns, each square represents 1″ (2.5 cm.). To enlarge the patterns, take a piece of brown paper or any other thickish paper as this will be your permanent pattern. Now draw on it a 1″ (2.5 cm.) grid—that is, horizontal lines 1″ apart and vertical lines 1″ apart. Then copy your patterns onto the grid square by square and they will be the correct size.

When you have copied the patterns, including sewing lines, etcetera, trace them onto tissue paper and use the tissue paper patterns for cutting out the fabric. (It is easier to use the tissue because you can see through it.)

A NOTE ABOUT MEASUREMENTS

Following all measurements, we have included centimeters (cm.) or millimeters (mm.) in anticipation of a changeover to the metric system.

Two: *UPSIDE-DOWN DOLLS*

Cinderella, Stepmother and Stepsisters

ONE DAY THERE came news of a big party to be given at the royal palace. It was to last three days and nights and the king had invited all the young ladies in the kingdom so that his son, a young and handsome prince, might choose one of them for his future bride.

Cinderella, Stepmother and Stepsisters

MATERIALS YOU'LL NEED

¾ yard (67.5 cm.) brown cotton material—Cinderella's, stepmother's and stepsisters' heads-and-bodies (C-1, C-2, S-1, S-2, M-1, M-2)

½ yard (45 cm.) light color sheath-lining material—Cinderella's skirt and blouse (C-3, C-4)

½ yard (45 cm.) solid color cotton material—stepmother's and stepsisters' skirt

½ yard (45 cm.) dark color sheath-lining material—Cinderella's coat (C-5, C-6, C-7, C-8)

¼ yard (22.5 cm.) of three different cotton print materials—stepmother's and stepsisters' blouses (S-3, S-4, S-5)

7 yards (630 cm.) lace—Cinderella's coat and blouse, stepmother's and stepsisters' blouses and skirt

1 yard (90 cm.) ribbon—Cinderella's coat and hair

8-ounce skein of black baby yarn—Cinderella's and one stepsister's hair

4-ounce skein of gray baby yarn—stepmother's hair

4-ounce skein of brown baby yarn—other stepsister's hair

Black, red, and brown embroidery floss for faces

1½ pounds of polyester fiberfill for stuffing

Note: All seam allowances are ½" (1.25 cm.) for dolls, and ¼" (6 mm.) for clothes.

CUTTING

Cinderella's head-and-body and clothes:

Make the paper patterns from the pattern pieces (C-1 through C-8), enlarging, if needed, to actual size. Cut all pattern pieces from material, remembering to reverse the pattern when pairs are needed.

For Cinderella's skirt, cut a rectangle 36 x 12" (90 x 30 cm.), and a strip 11 x 1¾" (27.5 x 4.5 cm.) for the waistband.

Stepmother's and Stepsisters' heads-and-bodies and clothes:

Make the paper patterns from the pattern pieces (M-1, M-2, S-1 through S-5), enlarging, if needed, to actual size. Cut all pattern pieces from material, remembering to reverse the pattern when pairs are needed.

For the stepmother's and stepsisters' skirt, cut a rectangle 36 x 12" (90 x 30 cm.), and a strip 11 x 1¾" (27.5 x 4.5 cm.) for the waistband.

For the stepmother's and stepsisters' blouses, cut 6 strips 3½ x ½" (8.75 x 1.25 cm.) for the cuffs. They should match the blouse materials.

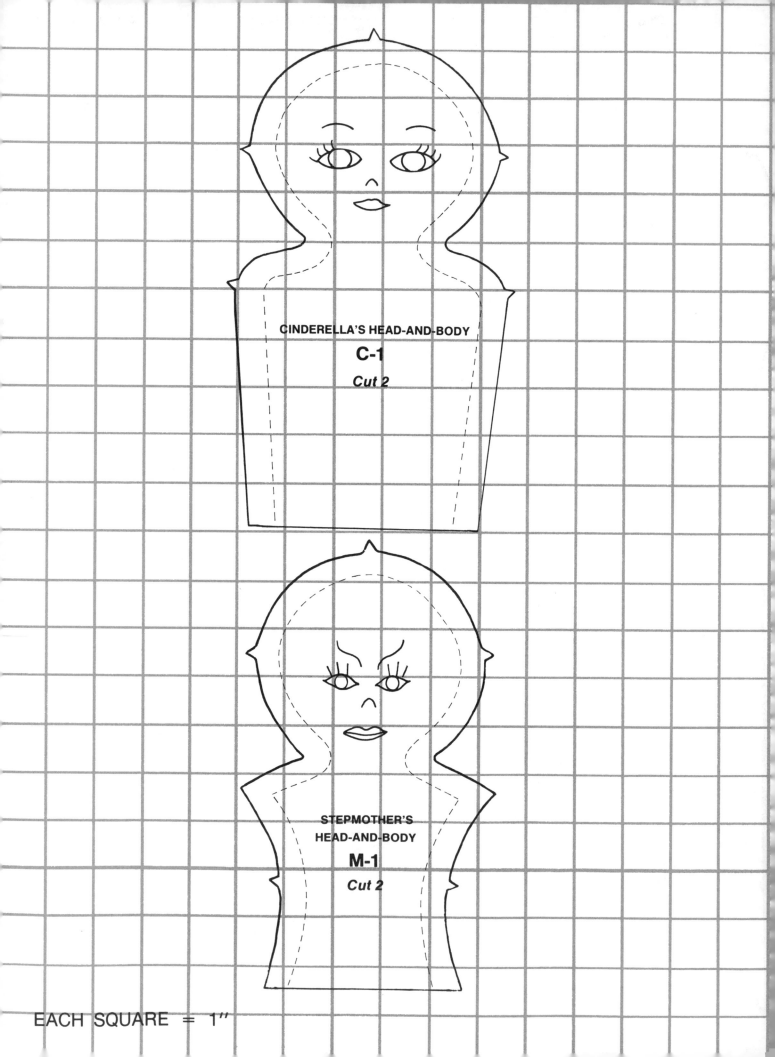

CINDERELLA'S HEAD-AND-BODY

C-1

Cut 2

STEPMOTHER'S
HEAD-AND-BODY

M-1

Cut 2

EACH SQUARE = 1"

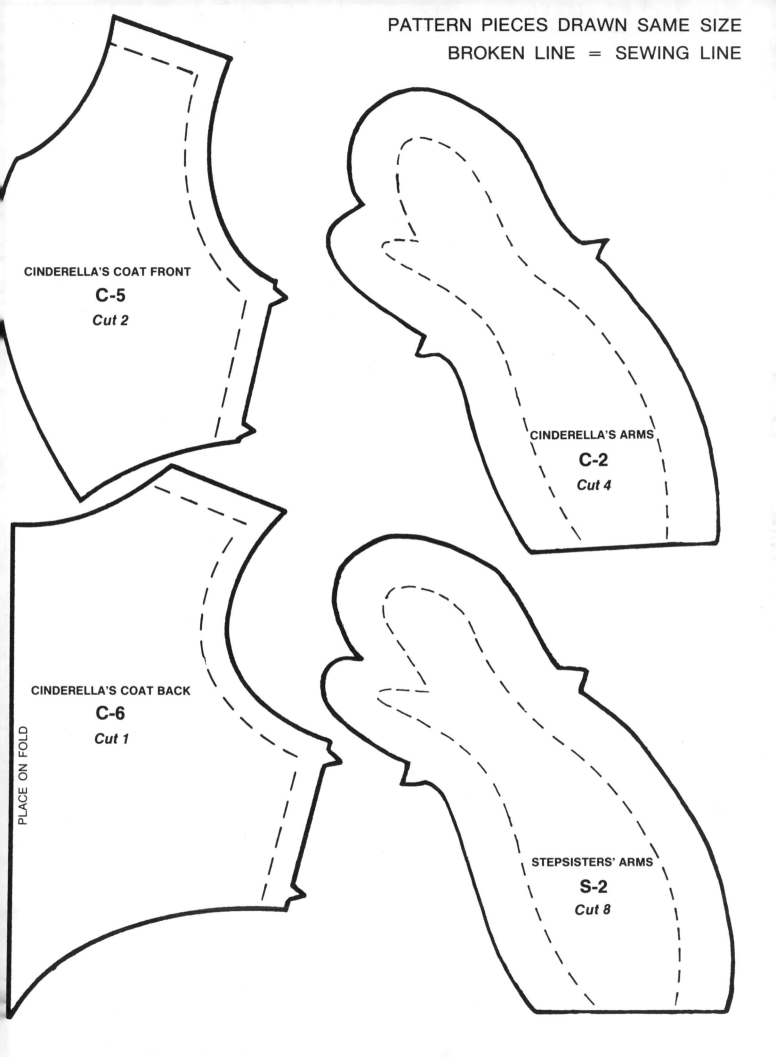

PATTERN PIECES DRAWN SAME SIZE
BROKEN LINE = SEWING LINE

CINDERELLA'S COAT FRONT
C-5
Cut 2

CINDERELLA'S ARMS
C-2
Cut 4

CINDERELLA'S COAT BACK
C-6
Cut 1

PLACE ON FOLD

STEPSISTERS' ARMS
S-2
Cut 8

PATTERN PIECES DRAWN SAME SIZE

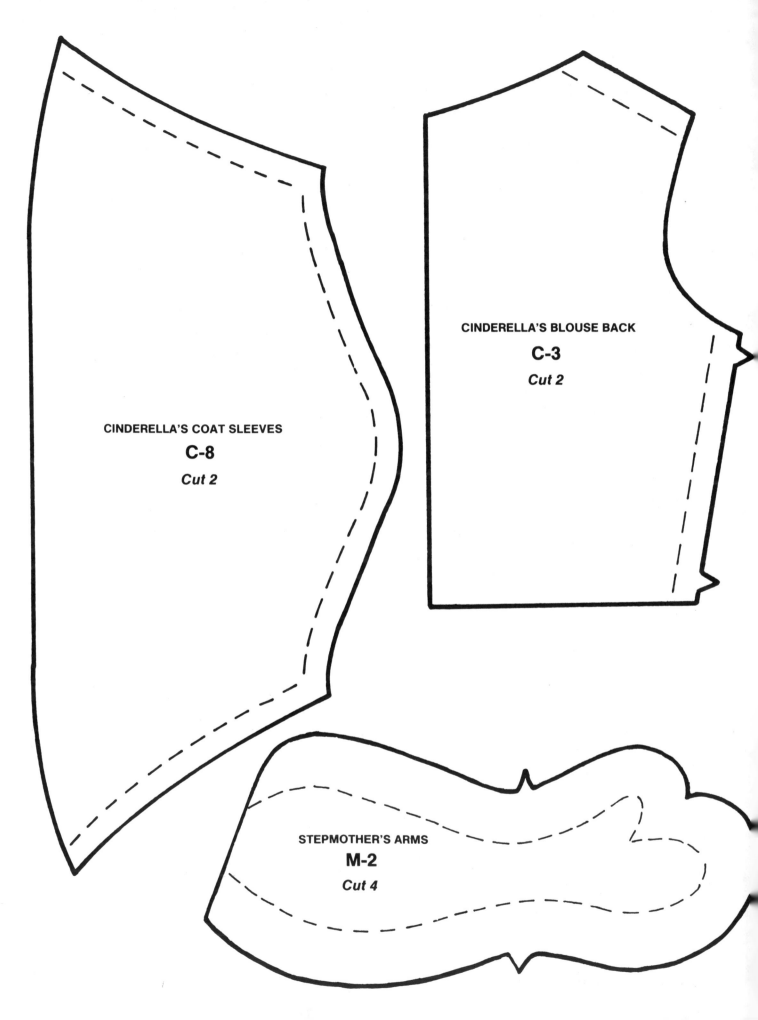

CINDERELLA'S COAT SLEEVES
C-8
Cut 2

CINDERELLA'S BLOUSE BACK
C-3
Cut 2

STEPMOTHER'S ARMS
M-2
Cut 4

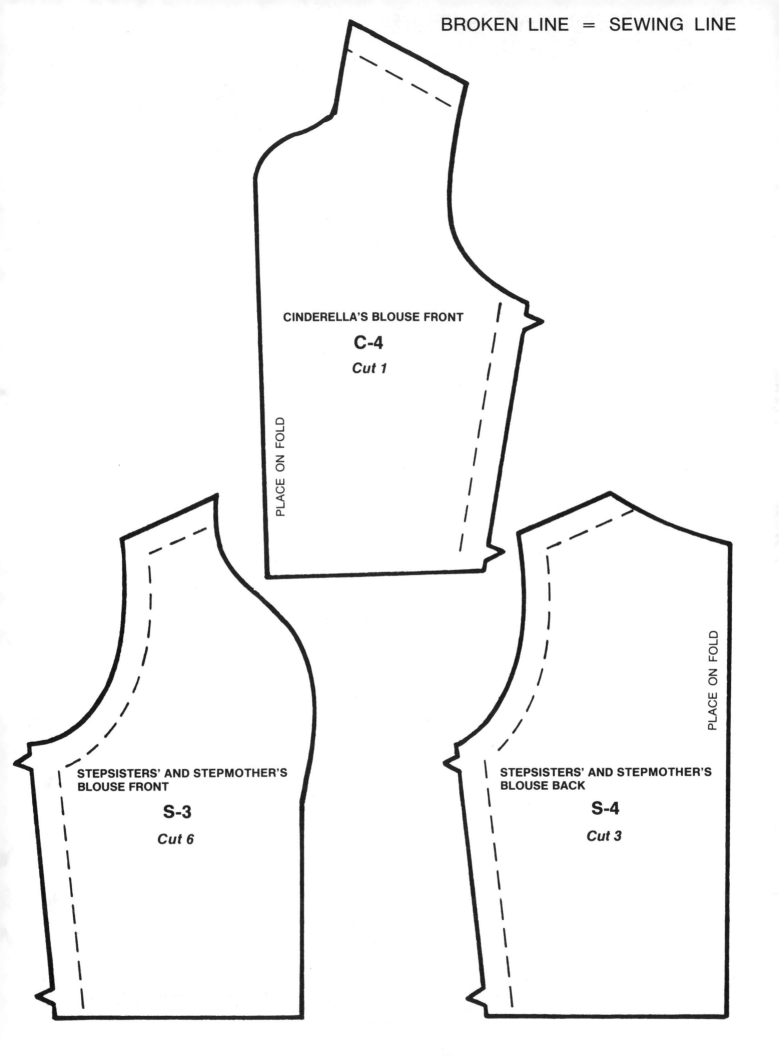

BROKEN LINE = SEWING LINE

CINDERELLA'S BLOUSE FRONT

C-4

Cut 1

PLACE ON FOLD

STEPSISTERS' AND STEPMOTHER'S
BLOUSE FRONT

S-3

Cut 6

STEPSISTERS' AND STEPMOTHER'S
BLOUSE BACK

S-4

Cut 3

PLACE ON FOLD

PATTERN PIECES DRAWN SAME SIZE
BROKEN LINE = SEWING LINE

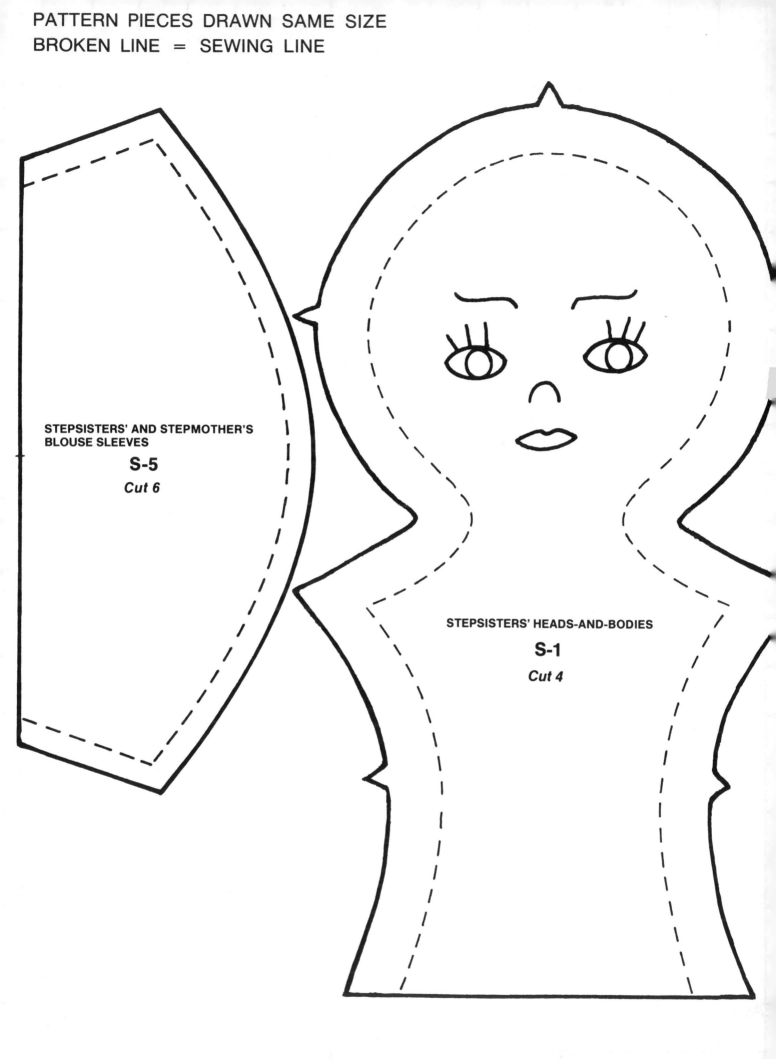

STEPSISTERS' AND STEPMOTHER'S
BLOUSE SLEEVES

S-5

Cut 6

STEPSISTERS' HEADS-AND-BODIES

S-1

Cut 4

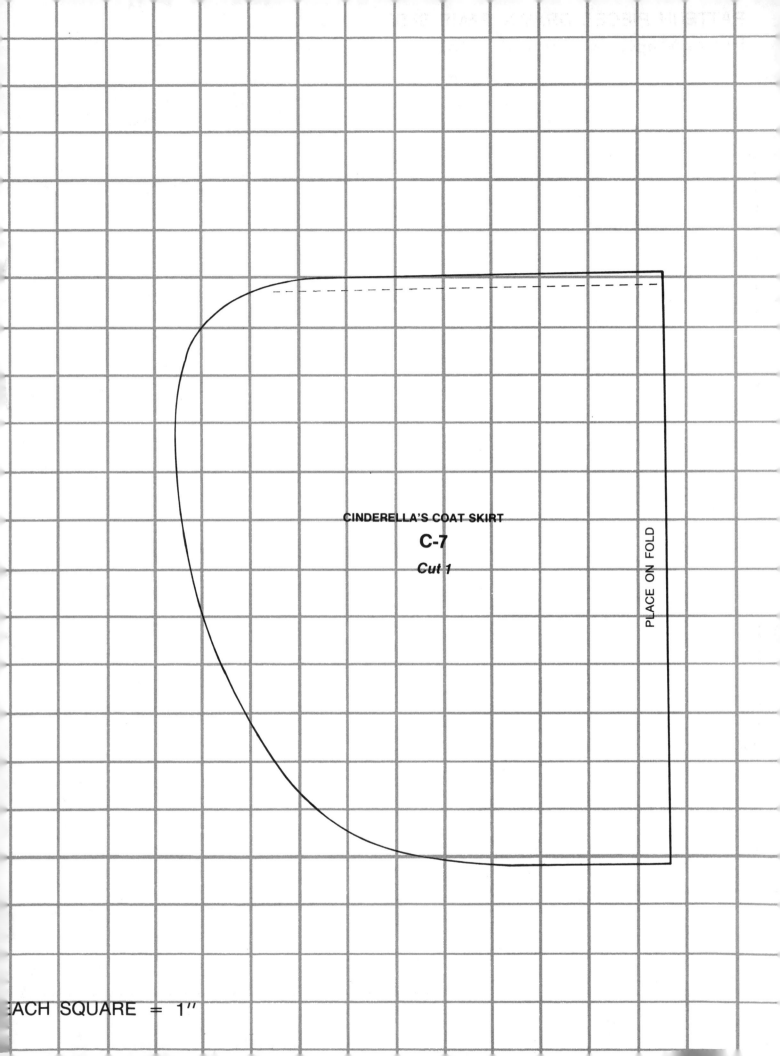

CINDERELLA'S COAT SKIRT

C-7

Cut 1

PLACE ON FOLD

EACH SQUARE = 1"

SEWING AND EMBROIDERING

Cinderella's face:

Using the face drawing (Fig. 1) as a guide, draw Cinderella's face with a pencil onto one of the head-and-body sections. Then, using an embroidery hoop, embroider the features with a single strand of embroidery floss. Use red for the nose and mouth, working in an outline stitch. Use black for the eyes, eyebrows, eyelashes and irises. The eyes and eyebrows are worked in an outline stitch, the eyelashes in a straight stitch. The irises are worked in a satin stitch.

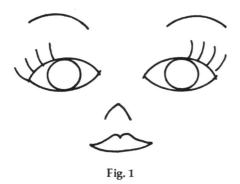

Fig. 1

Cinderella's head-and-body

Match the notches and baste the head-and-body sections (C-1) together, right sides facing. Machine-stitch where indicated on the pattern, leaving the bottom open for stuffing. Remove basting thread. Trim the seams and clip the neck curves as illustrated. (Fig. 2).

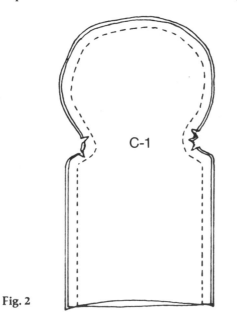

Fig. 2

Turn the material right side out and stuff with polyester fiberfill, packing it until the body is very, very stiff. Then hand-stitch the opening with heavy-duty thread, using a whip stitch.

Cinderella's arms:

Match the notches and baste two arm sections (C-2) together, right sides facing. Machine-stitch where indicated on the pattern, leaving the bottom open for stuffing. Remove basting thread. Trim the seams and clip the corners. (Fig. 3). Repeat with other

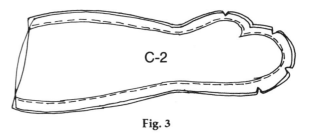

Fig. 3

arm. Turn the material right side out and stuff as above. Turn in the opening and whip-stitch the arms to the body with heavy-duty thread. (Fig. 4).

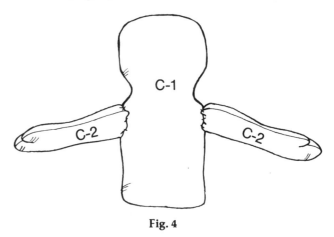

Fig. 4

Stepmother's face:

Using the face drawing (Fig. 5) as a guide, draw the stepmother's face with a pencil onto one of the head-and-body sections (M-1). Then, using an embroidery hoop, embroider the features with a single strand of embroidery floss. Use red for the nose and mouth, working in an outline stitch. Use black for the eyes, eyebrows, eyelashes and irises. The

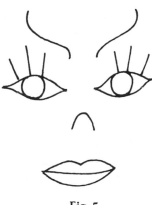

Fig. 5

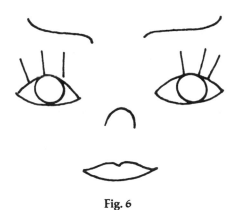

Fig. 6

eyes and eyebrows are worked in an outline stitch, the eyelashes in a straight stitch. The irises are worked in a buttonhole stitch.

Stepmother's head-and-body:

Match the notches and baste the head-and-body sections (M-1) together, right sides facing. Machine-stitch where indicated on the pattern, leaving the bottom open for stuffing. Remove basting thread. Trim the seams and clip the neck curves. Turn the material right side out and stuff with polyester fiberfill, packing it until the body is very, very stiff. Then hand-stitch the opening with heavy-duty thread, using a whip stitch.

Stepmother's arms:

Match the notches and baste the arm sections (M-2) together, right sides facing. Machine-stitch where indicated on the pattern, leaving the bottom open for stuffing. Remove basting thread. Trim the seams and clip the corners. Repeat with other arm. Turn the material right side out and stuff as above. Turn in the opening and whip-stitch the arms to the body with heavy-duty thread.

Stepsisters' faces:

Using the face drawing (Fig. 6) as a guide, draw one stepsister's face with a pencil onto one of the head-and-body sections (S-1). Then, using an embroidery hoop, embroider the features with a single strand of embroidery floss. Use red for the nose and mouth, working in an outline stitch. Use black for the eyes, eyebrows, eyelashes and irises. The eyes and eyebrows are worked in an outline stitch, the eyelashes in a straight stitch. The irises are worked in a buttonhole stitch. Repeat with other sister.

Stepsisters' heads-and-bodies:

Match the notches and baste one embroidered head-and-body section to a plain head-and-body section (S-1), right sides facing. Machine-stitch where indicated on the pattern, leaving the bottom open for stuffing. Remove basting thread. Trim the seams and clip the neck curves. Turn the material right side out and stuff with polyester fiberfill, packing it until the body is very, very stiff. Then hand-stitch the opening with heavy-duty thread, using a whip stitch. Repeat with the other sister.

Stepsisters' arms:

Match the notches and baste two arm sections (S-2) together, right sides facing. Machine-stitch where indicated on the pattern, leaving the bottom open for stuffing. Remove basting thread. Trim the seams and clip the corners. Repeat with other arms. Turn the material right side out and stuff as above. Turn in the opening and whip-stitch the arms to the bodies with heavy-duty thread.

HAIR

Cinderella:

To make the bangs, wind black yarn 35 times around a 4 x 1½" (10 x 3.75 cm.) piece of cardboard. Use the 1½" (3.75 cm.) side for looping. (Fig. 7). Machine-stitch at ¼" (6

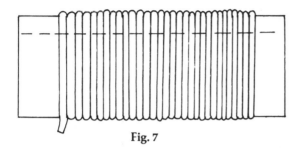

Fig. 7

mm.) depth along one of the 4" (10 cm.) ends and remove the cardboard. Then hand-stitch the bangs to the forehead of the doll. (Fig. 8).

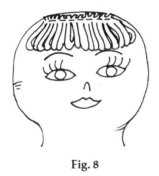

Fig. 8

For the body of the hair, place ten pins across the back of the head and ten pins 2" (5 cm.) below the shoulders as shown in illustration. (Fig. 9). Wind black yarn from top to

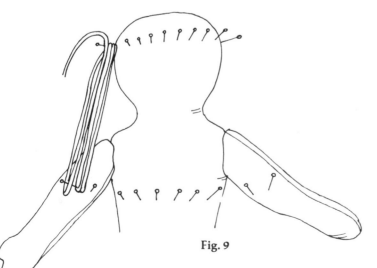

Fig. 9

bottom 10 times around each end pin but only 8 times around the middle pins. (Fig. 9). Then thread a needle with the same yarn and hand-stitch the yarn to the head across the top and at the base of the neck. Remove the pins. (Fig. 10).

Fig. 10

Finally, wind some more black yarn 35 times around a 6 x 4" (15 x 10 cm.) piece of cardboard. Use the 6" (15 cm.) side for looping. Machine-stitch at ½" (1.25 cm.) depth across one of the 4" (10 cm.) ends and remove the cardboard. Hand-stitch yarn to the forehead at the top seam of the doll, covering the ends of the bangs. Flip the yarn over and tie at the back with yarn and a ribbon. (Fig. 11).

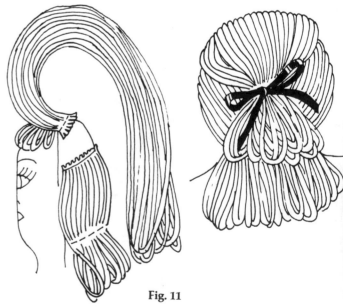

Fig. 11

Stepmother:

Wind gray yarn 35 times around a 4 x 10″ (10 x 25 cm.) piece of cardboard, looping around the 10″ (25 cm.) side. Remove the cardboard, and cut the loops on one side. Machine-stitch across the yarn at the other end. You should now have 10″ (25 cm.) of yarn on either side of the machine stitching. Place the yarn on the doll as shown in illustration. (Fig. 12). The stitching on the yarn should be on the forehead, about ½″ (1.25 cm.) below the seam of the doll.

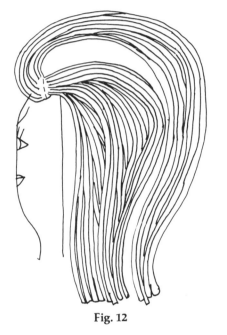

Fig. 12

Thread a needle with the same yarn and stitch across, securing the yarn to the forehead. Then flip the yarn over and hand-stitch at the back base of the neck. (Fig. 13). Pull the excess yarn up again, turn the ends under and hand-stitch at the top, as shown in illustration. (Fig. 13). Make sure it is secure.

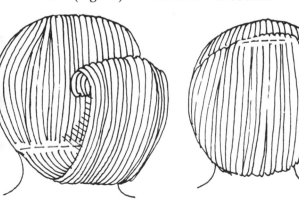

Fig. 13

Stepsisters:

The hair for the stepsisters is done exactly like the stepmother's (Figs. 12 and 13). Use black yarn for one stepsister and brown yarn for the other stepsister.

MAKING THE CLOTHES

Cinderella's blouse:

Baste and machine-stitch the two sections of the back (C-3) to the front (C-4) at the shoulders, right sides facing. Turn under the edges at the armholes and the neck and add lace by machine-stitching. The lace at the neck should be standing up. Then match the notches, and baste and machine-stitch the side seams. Remove all basting thread. Hem the back sections. Put the blouse aside until the dolls have been joined.

Cinderella's coat:

Baste and machine-stitch the two sections of the coat front (C-5) to the coat back (C-6) at the shoulders, right sides facing. Next take the sleeves (C-8) and turn under the raw edges at the cuffs (the side with no seam line on the pattern). Gather lace by hand and machine-stitch to the right sides of the cuffs. Set in the sleeves at the armholes, baste and machine-stitch. (Fig. 14). Then baste the side

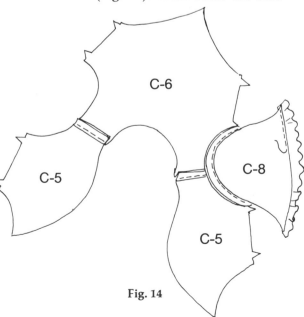

Fig. 14

seams of the sleeves and machine-stitch. Match the notches of the front sections with the back, baste and machine-stitch down the sides. Remove all basting thread.

Next take the coat skirt (C-7) and gather at the seam line marked on the pattern. Pull to shape so that it matches the bottom of the coat top. Then baste and machine-stitch the coat skirt to the coat top. Remove basting thread. Now turn under the raw edges of the coat, all the way from the neck and around the bottom and back up on the other side to the neck again. Baste. Gather lace by hand and machine-stitch it to the basted edges, as shown in illustration. (Fig. 15). Remove basting thread. Finish by adding two 14″ (35 cm.) ribbons at the waist of the coat. Put the coat aside.

Cinderella's and Stepmother's/Stepsisters' skirts:

The skirts for Cinderella, the stepmother and the stepsisters are made together. With right sides facing, pin the cotton material to the sheath-lining material at the hemline, or along the 36″ (90 cm.) edge. Leave a ¼″ (6 mm.) seam and baste it. Remove pins. Machine-stitch the sections together along the hemline. (Fig. 16). Remove basting thread.

Machine-stitch gathering stitches on the other two 36″ (90 cm.) edges, but don't pull to shape as yet. Fold the fabric in half with the right sides facing so that the piece now measures 23½ x 18″ (58.75 x 45 cm.) and baste along the 23½″ (58.75 cm.) edge. (The previously stitched seam now faces itself.) Measure 2″ (5 cm.) in from each end—along basted edge—and mark with pins. (Fig. 17). Next, machine-stitch between these pin marks, back-stitching at the beginning and end to secure the seam. Remove pins and basting thread.

Fig. 15

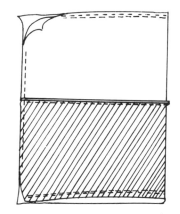

Fig. 17

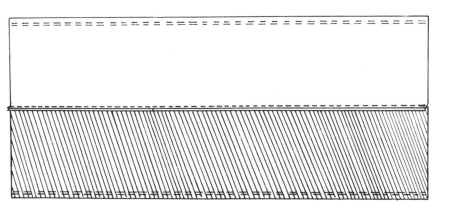

Fig. 16

Now turn this tubular piece inside out, wrong sides facing, and match the top raw edges as shown in illustration. (Fig. 18). Top-

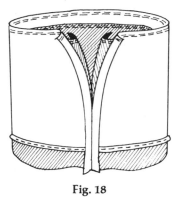

Fig. 18

stitch along the hemline. Add a border of lace to the solid cotton material at the hemline. The raw edges become the skirt waistlines. The seams become the center backs of the skirts.

Cinderella's and Stepmother's/ Stepsisters' waistbands:

With right sides facing, fold the cotton waistband strip—11 x 1¾″ (27.5 x 4.5 cm.)—in half lengthwise and machine-stitch each end. Back-stitch to make them secure. Next, turn the piece to the right side and press. Pull to shape the top raw edge of the cotton skirt to fit the waistband. Turn under one right side raw edge of the band and pin to the right side top raw edge of the cotton skirt, matching each end with the center-back seam of the skirt. Baste, remove pins and machine-stitch. Remove basting thread.

Flip the waistband over the top of the skirt and, turning under the remaining raw edge of the band, hemstitch it to the other side to encase the top raw edge of the same skirt. (Fig. 19). Repeat this procedure with the

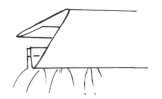

Fig. 19

sheath-lining waistband to encase the top raw edge of the sheath-lining skirt at the waist. Put aside.

Stepmother's and Stepsisters' blouses:

All three blouses are made the same way. First, make a tuck in the center of the back (S-4) at the neck edge. Baste and machine-stitch the back to the two sections of the front (S-3) at the shoulders, right sides facing. Next, gather the sleeves (S-5) at the cuff edges so that they now measure 3½″ (8.75 cm.). Then add the cuffs in the same way as the waistband is added to the skirt. Now gather the sleeves at the armhole edges to fit the armholes. Set in the sleeves, baste and machine-stitch.

Next, turn under the raw edges of the neck and the front sections, baste and add lace by machine-stitching. (Fig. 20). The lace

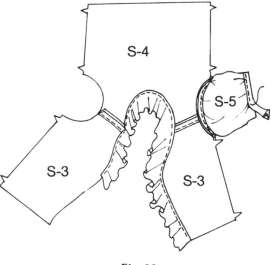

Fig. 20

should be machine-stitched to the wrong side so that it stands up. Baste and machine-stitch the side seams of the sleeves and then, matching the notches of the back to the front sections baste and machine-stitch down the sides. Remove all basting thread. Put blouses on dolls, crossing the material over in front. Hemstitch the fronts closed.

DOLL ASSEMBLY

First, the stepmother and the two stepsisters are stitched together. Hook the arms under each other and tie a ribbon around them to hold them in place while stitching. Make sure the heads are level. Hand-stitch them at the bottom first and then through the shoulders. Make sure the stitches do not show too much on the blouses. Then turn Cinderella in the same direction as the stepmother. (Fig. 21). Using heavy-duty thread and the whip stitch, hand-stitch Cinderella to her family firmly at the waist so that the doll does not bend. Now stitch the stepmother's and the stepsisters' blouses down at the waists.

FINISHING

Put the blouse on Cinderella and hemstitch up the back, closing the opening and stitching it to the doll at the same time. Then put the skirt on the stepmother and the stepsisters. The seam should be at the back. Hand-stitch the waistband to the dolls and hand-stitch the skirt's seam closed. Turn the dolls upside down and hand-stitch the other waistband to Cinderella. Hand-stitch the skirt's seam closed. Put on Cinderella's coat.

Fig. 21

Little Boy Blue
and the Sheep

LITTLE BOY BLUE, *come blow your horn;*
The sheep's in the meadow, the cow's in the corn.
But where is the boy who looks after the sheep?
He's under a haycock, fast asleep.

Little Boy Blue
and the Sheep

MATERIALS YOU'LL NEED

¼ yard (22.5 cm.) unbleached muslin—Boy Blue's head-and-body (B-1, B-2)

½ yard (45 cm.) white terry cloth—sheep's head-and-body (S-1, S-2)

2 pieces of black felt, each 9 x 12″ (22.5 x 30 cm.)—sheep's legs, ears and muzzle (S-3, S-4, S-5, S-6)

A scrap of gray felt—hoofs, eyes (S-7, S-8)

A scrap of pink felt—sheep's tongue

A 9 x 12″ (22.5 x 30 cm.) piece of gold felt—Boy Blue's horn (B-12)

¼ yard (22.5 cm.) red cotton material—Boy Blue's cap (B-3, B-4)

¼ yard (22.5 cm.) white cotton material—Boy Blue's shirt (B-5, B-6, B-7, B-8)

¼ yard (22.5 cm.) blue cotton material—Boy Blue's overalls (B-9, B-10, B-11)

1 yard (90 cm.) gold cotton material—double skirt for Boy Blue and sheep

4-ounce skein of gold yarn—hay

4-ounce skein of dark brown yarn—Boy Blue's hair

2 small white buttons

Black, red, and gray embroidery floss for faces

Sewing thread and heavy-duty thread to match materials

1½ pounds of polyester fiberfill for stuffing

Note: All seam allowances are ½″ (1.25 cm.) for dolls, and ¼″ (6 mm.) for clothes.

CUTTING

Boy Blue's head-and-body and clothes:

Make the paper patterns from the pattern pieces (B-1 through B-12), enlarging, if needed, to actual size. Cut all pattern pieces from material, remembering to reverse the pattern when pairs are needed.

For Boy Blue's skirt, cut a rectangle 36 x 12″ (90 x 30 cm.), and a strip 11 x 1¾″ (27.5 x 4.5 cm.) for the waistband.

Sheep's head-and-body and clothes:

Make the paper patterns from the pattern pieces (S-1 through S-8), enlarging, if needed, to actual size. Cut all pattern pieces from material, remembering to reverse the pattern when pairs are needed.

For the sheep's skirt, cut a rectangle 36 x 12″ (90 x 30 cm.), and a strip 11 x 1¾″ (27.5 x 4.5 cm.) for the waistband.

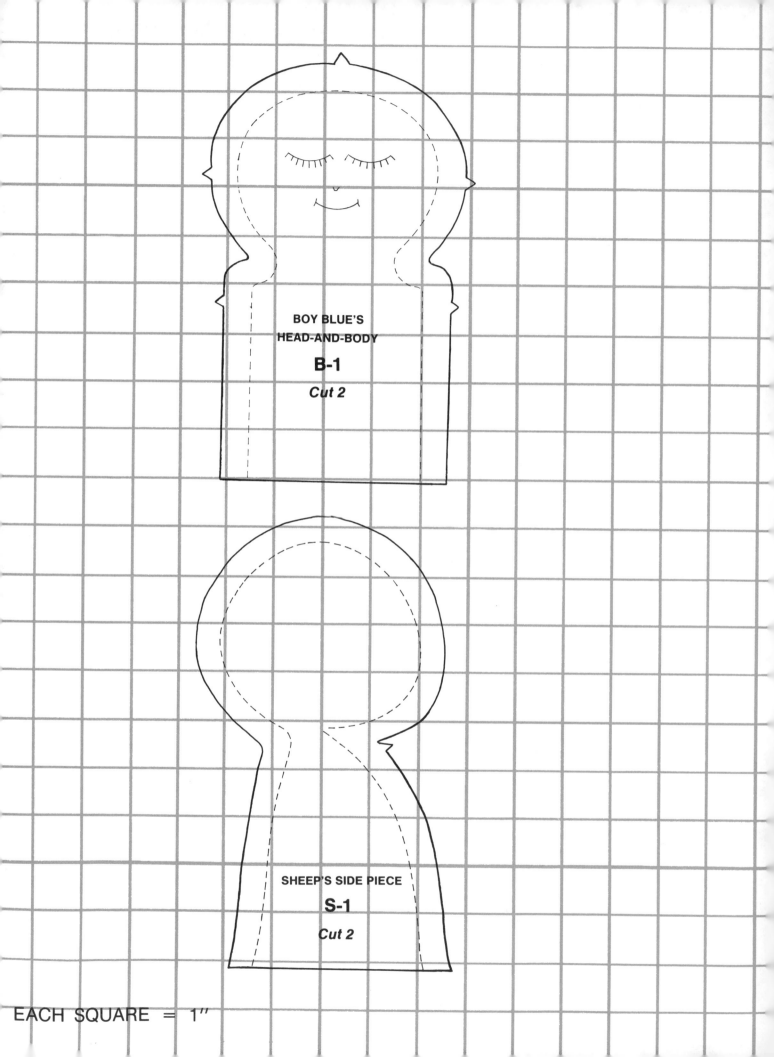

BOY BLUE'S
HEAD-AND-BODY
B-1
Cut 2

SHEEP'S SIDE PIECE
S-1
Cut 2

EACH SQUARE = 1"

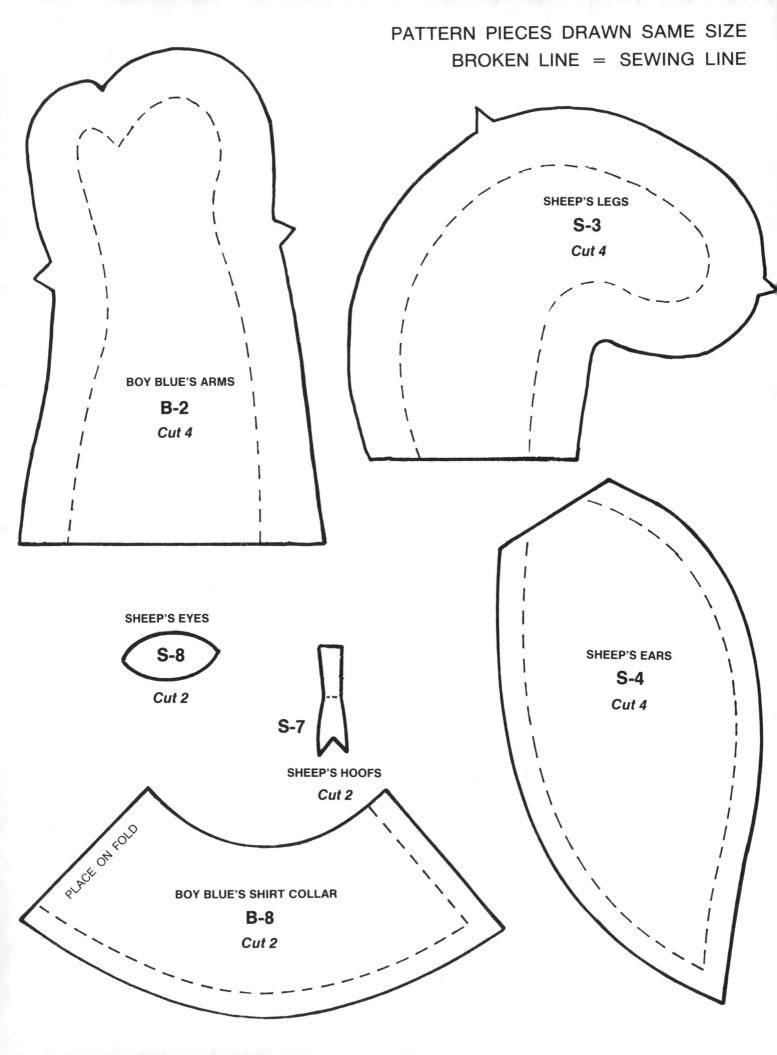

PATTERN PIECES DRAWN SAME SIZE
BROKEN LINE = SEWING LINE

SHEEP'S LEGS
S-3
Cut 4

BOY BLUE'S ARMS
B-2
Cut 4

SHEEP'S EYES
S-8
Cut 2

S-7

SHEEP'S HOOFS
Cut 2

SHEEP'S EARS
S-4
Cut 4

PLACE ON FOLD

BOY BLUE'S SHIRT COLLAR
B-8
Cut 2

PATTERN PIECES DRAWN SAME SIZE

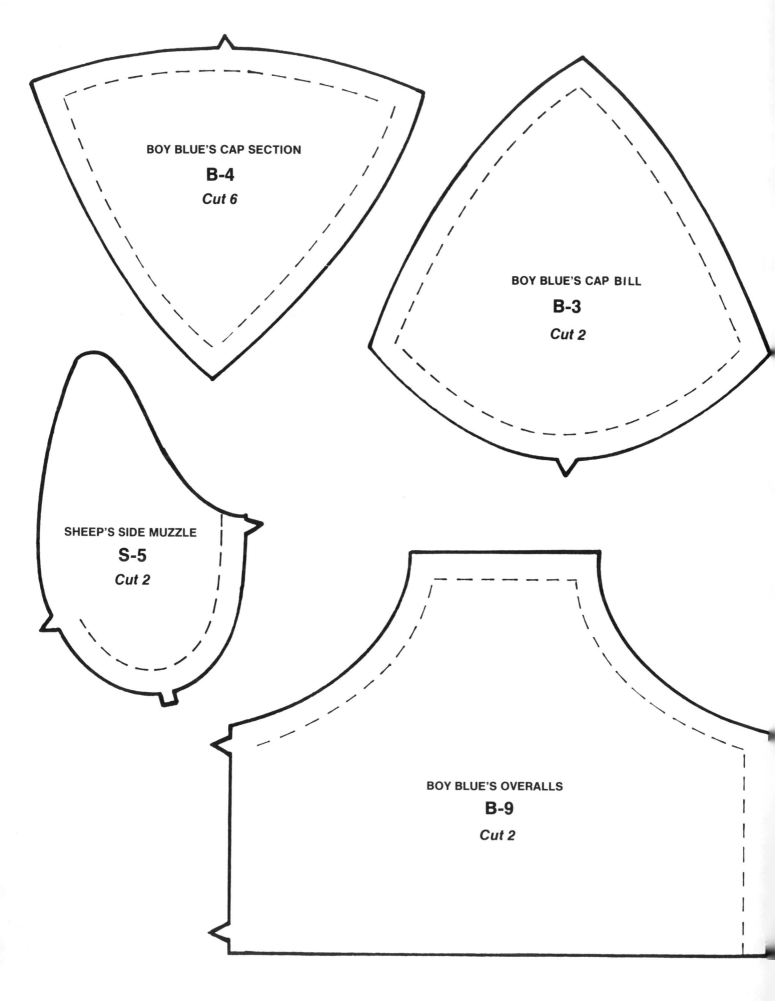

BOY BLUE'S CAP SECTION
B-4
Cut 6

BOY BLUE'S CAP BILL
B-3
Cut 2

SHEEP'S SIDE MUZZLE
S-5
Cut 2

BOY BLUE'S OVERALLS
B-9
Cut 2

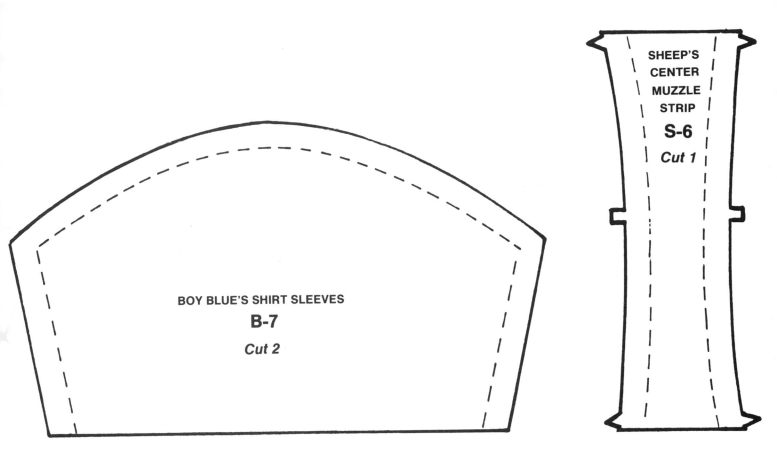

BOY BLUE'S SHIRT SLEEVES

B-7

Cut 2

SHEEP'S CENTER MUZZLE STRIP

S-6

Cut 1

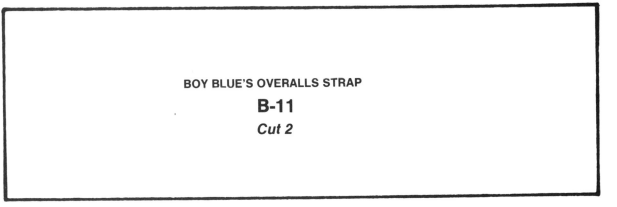

BOY BLUE'S OVERALLS STRAP

B-11

Cut 2

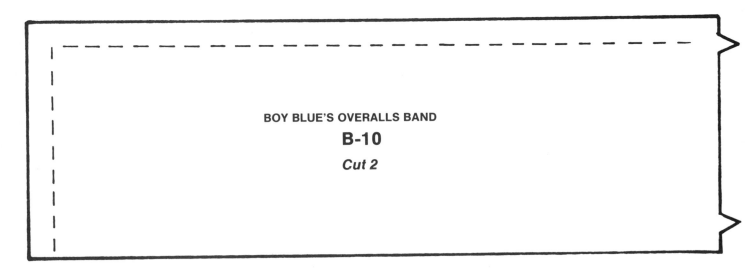

BOY BLUE'S OVERALLS BAND

B-10

Cut 2

PATTERN PIECES DRAWN SAME SIZE

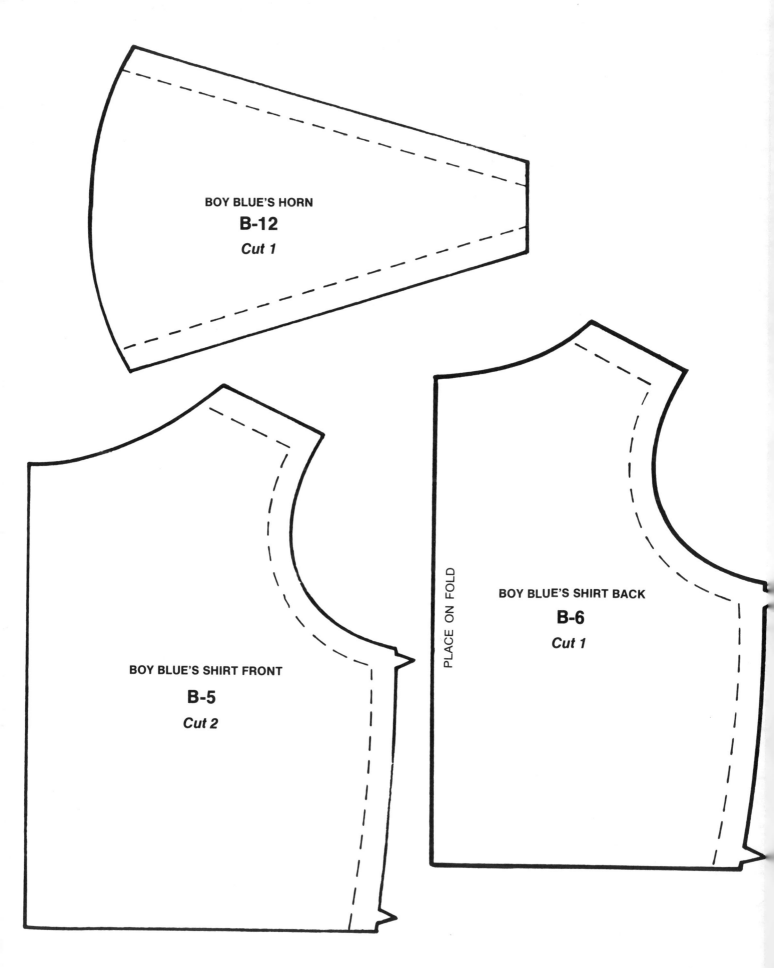

BOY BLUE'S HORN
B-12
Cut 1

BOY BLUE'S SHIRT FRONT
B-5
Cut 2

PLACE ON FOLD

BOY BLUE'S SHIRT BACK
B-6
Cut 1

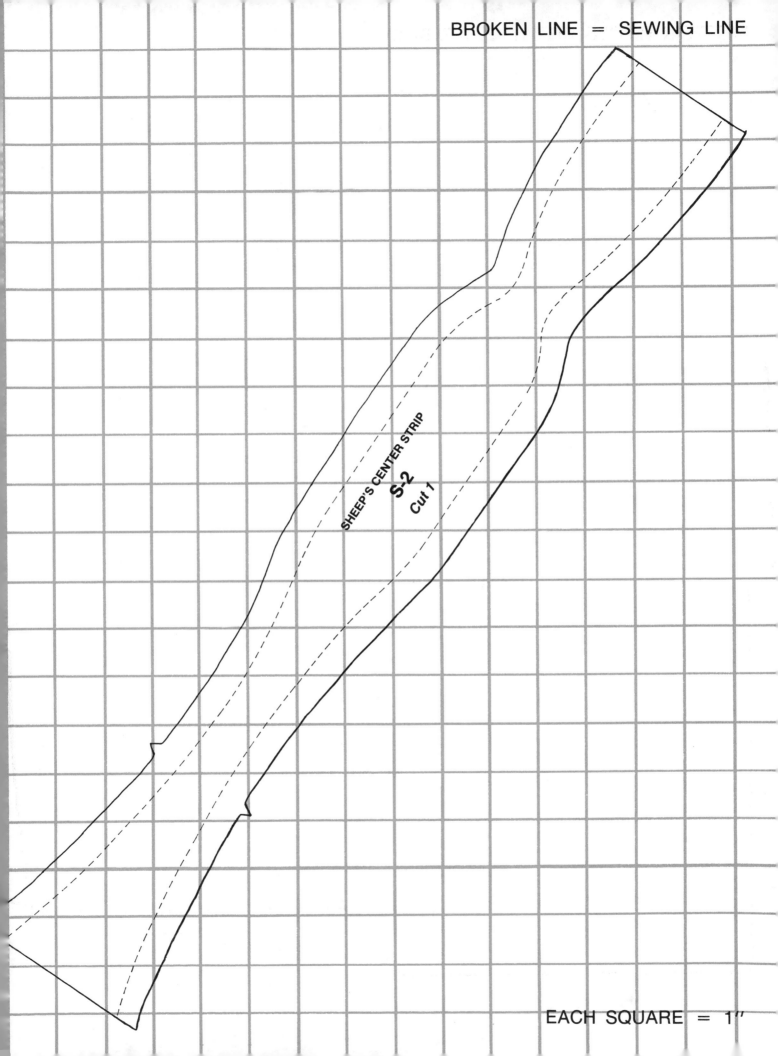

BROKEN LINE = SEWING LINE

SHEEP'S CENTER STRIP
S-2
Cut 1

EACH SQUARE = 1"

SEWING AND EMBROIDERING

Boy Blue's face:

Using the face drawing (Fig. 1) as a guide, draw Boy Blue's face with a pencil onto one of the head-and-body sections. Then, using an embroidery hoop, embroider the features with a single strand of embroidery floss. Use red for the nose and mouth, working in an outline stitch. Use black for the eyelashes, working in a straight stitch.

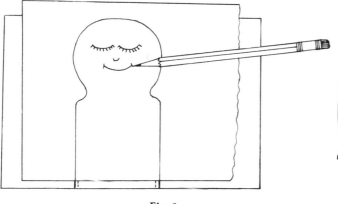

Fig. 1

Boy Blue's head-and-body:

Match the notches and baste the head-and-body sections (B-1) together, right sides facing. Machine-stitch where indicated on the pattern, leaving the bottom open for stuffing. Remove basting thread. Trim the seams and clip the neck curves as illustrated. (Fig. 2).

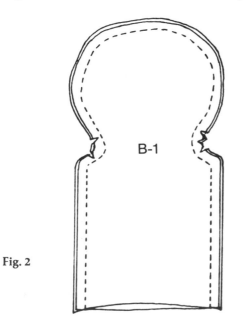

Fig. 2

Turn the material right side out and stuff with polyester fiberfill, packing it until the body is very very stiff. Then hand-stitch the opening with heavy-duty thread, using a whip stitch.

Boy Blue's arms:

Match the notches and baste two arm sections (B-2) together, right sides facing. Machine-stitch where indicated on the pattern, leaving the bottom open for stuffing. Remove basting thread. Trim the seams and clip the corners. (Fig. 3). Repeat with the

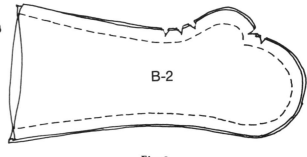

Fig. 3

other arm. Turn the material right side out and stuff as above. Turn in the opening and whip-stitch the arms to the body with heavy-duty thread. (Fig. 4).

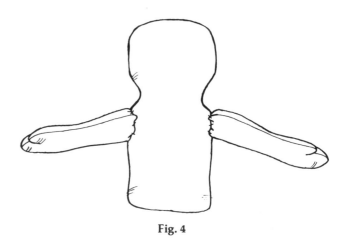

Fig. 4

Sheep's head-and-body:

Take one of the sheep's side pieces (S-1) and ease the sheep's center strip (S-2) around it. (Fig. 5). Pin and baste these together. Make

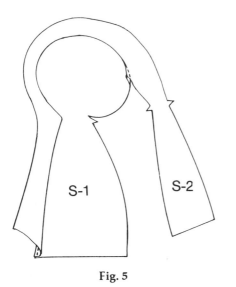

Fig. 5

Pin and baste all around, leaving the straight edge open for stuffing. Then remove pins, and machine-stitch, making sure the hoof has been stitched in. Remove basting thread. Trim the seams and clip the curves.

Then turn the material right side out and stuff with polyester fiberfill, packing it until the leg is very, very stiff. Repeat with the other leg. Finally, position both legs (Fig. 7) and hand-stitch to the body with heavy-duty thread, using a whip stitch.

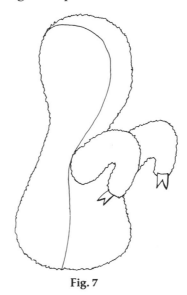

Fig. 7

sure the notch on the side piece matches with the notch on the center strip. Then remove pins and machine-stitch. Add the second side piece to the other side of the center strip in the same way.

Trim the seams and clip the curves. Remove all basting thread. Turn the material right side out and stuff with polyester fiberfill, packing it until the body is very, very stiff. Then hand-stitch the opening with heavy-duty thread, using a whip stitch.

Sheep's legs:

Insert one hoof (S-7) between two leg sections (S-3) as shown in illustration. (Fig. 6).

Sheep's muzzle:

Fold back the center muzzle strip (S-6) ¼" (6 mm.). The fold-back should be just below the square notches. Then cut the tongue from pink felt and position it as shown in illustration. (Fig. 8). Baste and machine-stitch across

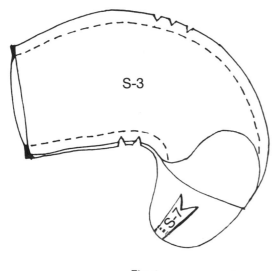

Fig. 6

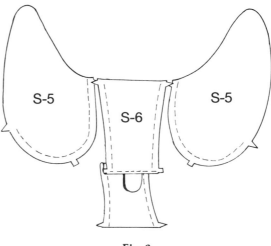

Fig. 8

the fold-back. Make sure the tongue has been stitched in.

Next, pin and baste the side muzzle sections (S-5) to the center strip, one on each side, as far as the triangular notches. (See Fig. 8.) Make sure that all the notches match. Now, remove pins and machine-stitch where basted. Remove basting thread. Trim the edges and clip the curves.

Stuff the muzzle lightly with polyester fiberfill and fit it over the snout of the sheep. Turn under the raw edges and hand-stitch muzzle in place. Mark the position of the nose and mouth, using the illustration (Fig. 9) as a guide. Embroider the facial details on the muzzle with two strands of gray embroidery floss.

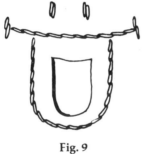

Fig. 9

Sheep's ears:

Baste two ear sections (S-4) together and machine-stitch where indicated on the pattern. Remove basting thread. Trim the seams and clip the curves. (Fig. 10). Repeat with the other ear. Then turn the material right side

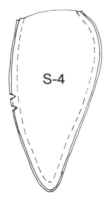

S-4

Fig. 10

out, turn under the raw edges, and hand-stitch the ears in line with the top seam of the sheep's head. (Fig. 11). Also hand-stitch ½" (1.25 cm.) down each side to keep the ears in place.

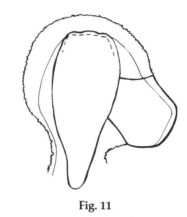

Fig. 11

Sheep's eyes:

Embroider the eyes (S-8) with black floss, working in a cross stitch. (Fig. 12). Then top-stitch the eyes in place.

Fig. 12

DOLL ASSEMBLY

When attaching the two parts together, turn Boy Blue in the opposite direction from the sheep. (Fig. 13). Using heavy-duty thread and the whip stitch, hand-stitch Boy Blue to the sheep firmly at the waist so that the doll does not bend.

Next, starting at the bottom and at the back of Boy Blue's head, arrange and stitch two rows of yarn. (Fig. 15). Then place the

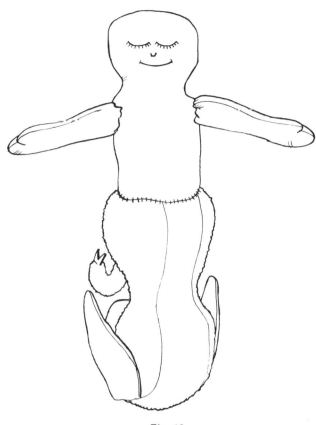

Fig. 13

HAIR

Boy Blue:

Take three 2 x 6" (5 x 15 cm.) pieces of cardboard and wind brown yarn approximately 40 times around each piece, looping around the 2" (5 cm.) side. Then machine-stitch along one 6" (15 cm.) end—at ¼" (6 mm.) depth from the edge—and cut the loops at the other end with scissors. (Fig. 14). Remove all the cardboard.

Fig. 14

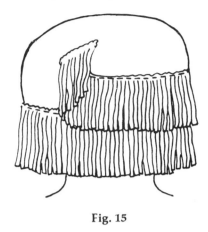

Fig. 15

third piece of the yarn at the crown of the head, the stitched edge doubled and forming a part. (Fig. 16). Stitch along the part and here and there to secure.

Fig. 16

MAKING THE CLOTHES

Boy Blue's cap:

Position the bill of the cap (B-3) and three of the other cap sections (B-4), right sides facing, with the notched sides forming the outer edge. Baste and machine-stitch them together. Repeat with the other B-3 and B-4 sections. Then baste and machine-stitch these two pieces around the outer edge as shown in illustration. (Fig. 17). Leave the B-3 side open. Remove all basting thread, and turn cap right side out. Top-stitch around the opening. Put aside.

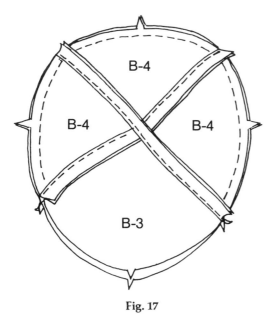

Fig. 17

Boy Blue's shirt:

Baste and machine-stitch the back (B-6) to the two sections of the front (B-5) at the shoulders, right sides facing. Then hem down both sections of the front.

Next take the two sections of the collar (B-8) and, with right sides facing, baste and machine-stitch them together where marked on the pattern. Clip the curves, remove basting thread and turn the collar. Turn under one raw edge of the collar and baste it to the right side of the shirt neck. Clip the curves. Then turn under the other raw edge of the collar and baste it to the other side of the shirt neck, as shown in illustration. (Fig. 18). Top-stitch across the basted edge and around the other edges of the collar.

Now take the sleeves (B-7) and hem along the straight edge. Then baste and machine-stitch the sleeves to the shirt, with the curved edge set at the armhole. (See Fig. 18). Next, baste and machine-stitch down the sleeves and, with notches matching, down the sides of the shirt. Remove all basting thread. Slip-stitch the shirt onto Boy Blue.

Boy Blue's overalls:

Baste and machine-stitch the overalls sections (B-9) together around the curved edges and on top. Right sides should be facing. Then take the two overalls band sections (B-10) and, with right sides facing, machine-stitch them together along one of the longer edges as marked on pattern. Then baste and machine-stitch the band to the overalls as shown in illustration. (Fig. 19). Remove basting thread and turn material right side out.

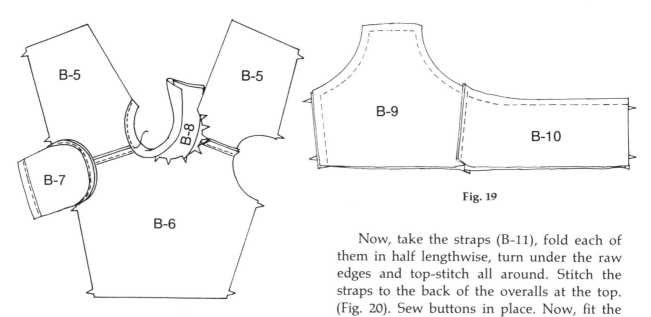

Fig. 18

Fig. 19

Now, take the straps (B-11), fold each of them in half lengthwise, turn under the raw edges and top-stitch all around. Stitch the straps to the back of the overalls at the top. (Fig. 20). Sew buttons in place. Now, fit the overalls on Boy Blue, taking the notched side

Fig. 20

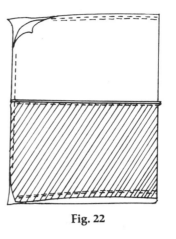

Fig. 22

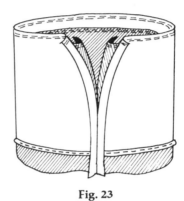

Fig. 23

of the band around the back. Turn under the raw edge of the band and hemstitch it to the notched side of the overalls. Cross the straps at the back and stitch the ends onto the band.

Boy Blue's and Sheep's skirts:

The skirts for Boy Blue and the sheep are made together. With right sides facing, pin the two sections of the gold cotton material together at the hemline, or along the 36″ (90 cm.) edge. Leave a ¼″ (6 mm.) seam and baste it. Remove pins. Machine-stitch the sections together along the hemline. (Fig. 21). Remove basting thread.

Machine-stitch gathering stitches on the other two 36″ (90 cm.) edges, but don't pull to shape as yet. Fold the fabric in half with the right sides facing so that the piece now measures 23½ x 18″ (58.75 x 45 cm.) and baste along the 23½″ (58.75 cm.) edge. (The previously stitched seam now faces itself.) Measure 2″ (5 cm.) in from each end—along basted edge—and mark with pins. (Fig. 22).

Next, machine-stitch between these pin marks, back-stitching at the beginning and end to secure the seam. Remove pins and basting thread.

Now turn this tubular piece inside out, wrong sides facing, and match the top raw edges as shown in illustration. (Fig. 23). Top-stitch along the hemline. The raw edges become the skirt waistlines. The seams become the center backs of the skirts.

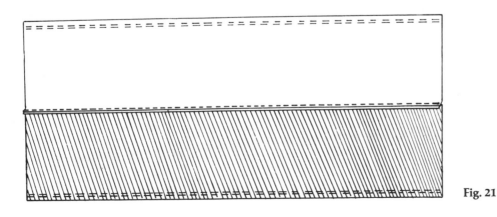

Fig. 21

Boy Blue's and Sheep's waistbands:

With right sides facing, fold one of the waistband strips—11 x 1¾" (27.5 x 4.5 cm.)—in half lengthwise and machine-stitch each end. Back-stitch to make them secure. Next, turn the piece to the right side and press. Pull to shape the top raw edge of one skirt to fit the waistband. Turn under one right side raw edge of the band and pin to the right side top raw edge of this skirt, matching each end with the center-back seam of the skirt. Baste, remove pins and machine-stitch. Remove basting thread.

Flip the waistband over the top of the skirt and, turning under the remaining raw edge of the band, hemstitch it to the other side to encase the top raw edge of the same skirt. (Fig. 24). Repeat this procedure with the other waistband to encase the top raw edge of the second skirt at the waist. Put aside.

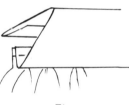

Fig. 24

Boy Blue's hay:

Wind gold yarn 120 times around a 10 x 10" (25 x 25 cm.) piece of cardboard. Then

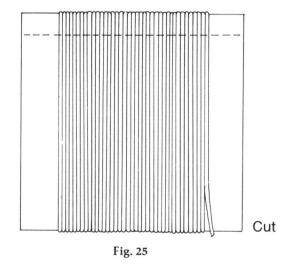

Fig. 25

machine-stitch about 1" (2.5 cm.) from one of the looped edges. (Fig. 25). Cut the loops at the other end. Hand-stitch the stitched edge onto the top of Boy Blue's skirt waistband. Make sure to leave 1" (2.5 cm.) on each side where the waistband is joined at the back.

Boy Blue's horn:

Fold the horn (B-12) in half lengthwise and machine-stitch where marked on pattern. Turn right side out and stuff a small amount of polyester fiberfill into the horn to establish its shape. For the handle, cut a piece of gold felt 2½ x ½" (6.75 x 1.25 cm.), double it lengthwise and top-stitch. Stitch the handle to the horn. (Fig. 26).

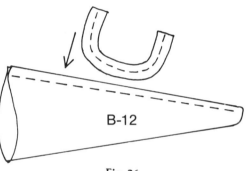

B-12

Fig. 26

FINISHING

Put the dress skirt on Boy Blue. The seam should be at the back. Hand-stitch the waistband to the doll and hand-stitch the skirt's seam closed. Place the cap on Boy Blue and stitch it to his head here and there to secure. Hand-stitch the horn to Boy Blue's right hand. Turn the doll upside down and hand-stitch the other waistband to the sheep. Hand-stitch the skirt's seam closed.

Little Red Riding Hood, Grandmother and the Wolf

ONCE UPON A TIME *a little girl had a red, hooded cloak her grandmother had given her. And she loved it so much and wore it so often that everyone called her Little Red Riding Hood.*

Little Red Riding Hood, Grandmother and the Wolf

MATERIALS YOU'LL NEED

½ yard (45 cm.) light pink cotton material—Red Riding Hood's and grandmother's heads-and-bodies, wolf's body (R-1, G-1, W-4)

⅛ yard (11.25 cm.) gray cotton material—wolf's head (W-1, W-2, W-3)

¼ yard (22.5 cm.) red corduroy—Red Riding Hood's cape (R-2, R-3)

¾ yard (67.5 cm.) red cotton print material—Red Riding Hood's skirt, blouse and cape lining (R-2 through R-6)

½ yard (45 cm.) dark cotton print material—grandmother's skirt, blouse and bonnet (R-4 through R-6 and G-2)

⅛ yard (11.25 cm.) white cotton material—grandmother's apron

1-ounce skein of yellow baby yarn—Red Riding Hood's hair

1 yard (90 cm.) gray rug yarn—grandmother's hair

1 yard (90 cm.) narrow red ribbon—Red Riding Hood's cape

1½ yards (135 cm.) narrow white ribbon—grandmother's bonnet and apron

⅓ yard (30 cm.) narrow red lace—Red Riding Hood's blouse

1 yard (90 cm.) narrow white lace—grandmother's blouse and bonnet

Elastic thread—grandmother's bonnet

Black, red, brown, and blue embroidery floss for faces

Sewing thread and heavy-duty thread to match materials

1½ pounds of polyester fiberfill for stuffing

Note: All seam allowances are ½" (1.25 cm.) for dolls, and ¼" (6 mm.) for clothes.

CUTTING

Red Riding Hood's head-and-body and clothes:

Make the paper patterns from the pattern pieces (R-1 through R-6), enlarging, if needed, to actual size. Cut all pattern pieces from material, remembering to reverse the pattern when pairs are needed.

For Red Riding Hood's skirt, cut a rectangle 36 x 9" (90 x 22.5 cm.), and a strip 10 x 1¾" (25 x 4.5 cm.) for the waistband.

Grandmother's and Wolf's head-and-body and clothes:

Make the paper patterns from the pattern pieces (G-1, G-2, W-1 through W-4), enlarging, if needed, to actual size. Cut all pattern pieces from material, remembering to reverse the pattern when pairs are needed.

For the grandmother's skirt, cut a rectangle 36 x 9" (90 x 22.5 cm.), and a strip 10 x 1¾" (25 x 4.5 cm.) for the waistband.

For the grandmother's apron cut a piece of white cotton material, 4 x 3" (10 x 7.5 cm.), either squared off or slightly rounded.

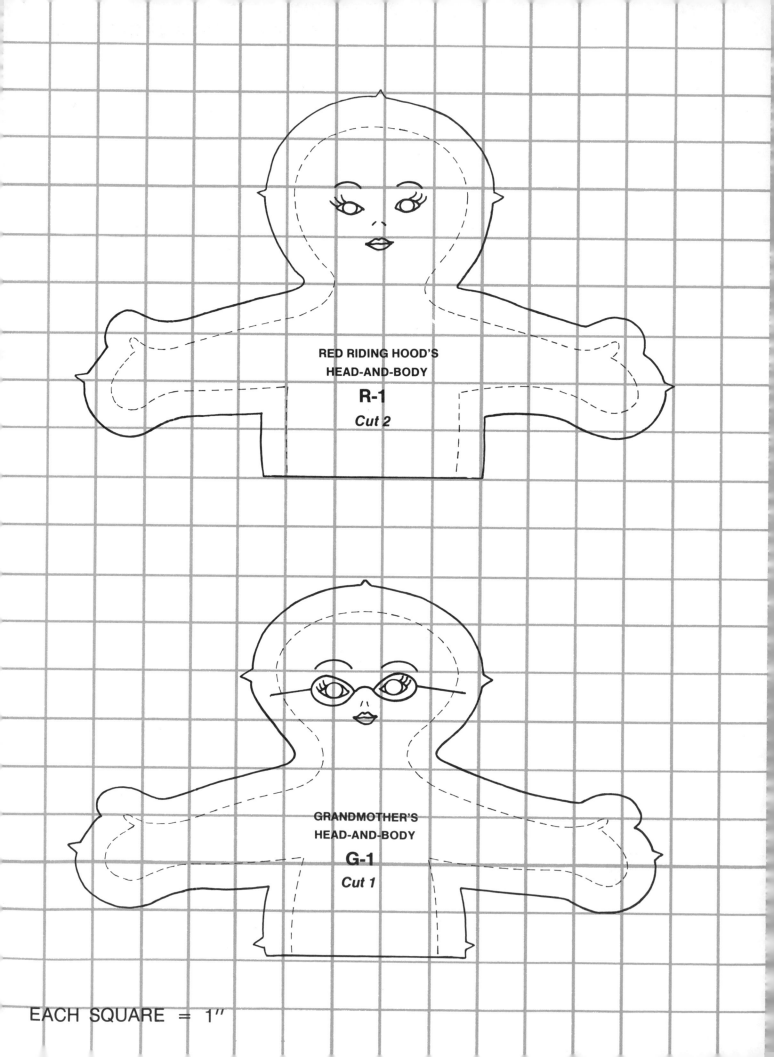

RED RIDING HOOD'S
HEAD-AND-BODY

R-1

Cut 2

GRANDMOTHER'S
HEAD-AND-BODY

G-1

Cut 1

EACH SQUARE = 1"

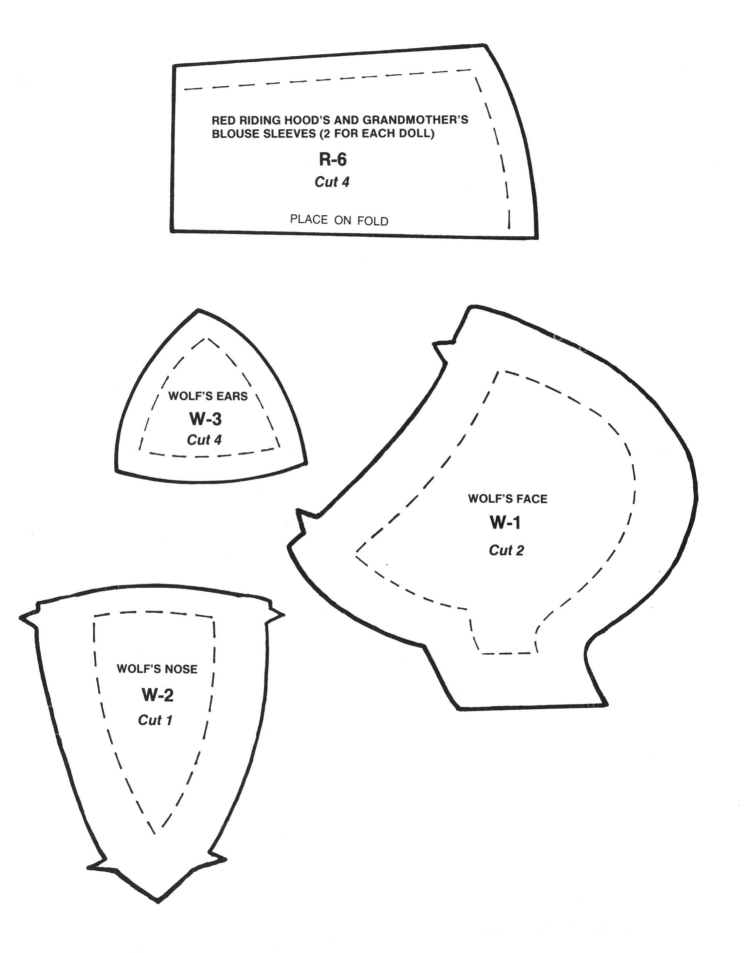

RED RIDING HOOD'S AND GRANDMOTHER'S
BLOUSE SLEEVES (2 FOR EACH DOLL)
R-6
Cut 4

PLACE ON FOLD

WOLF'S EARS
W-3
Cut 4

WOLF'S FACE
W-1
Cut 2

WOLF'S NOSE
W-2
Cut 1

PATTERN PIECES DRAWN SAME SIZE

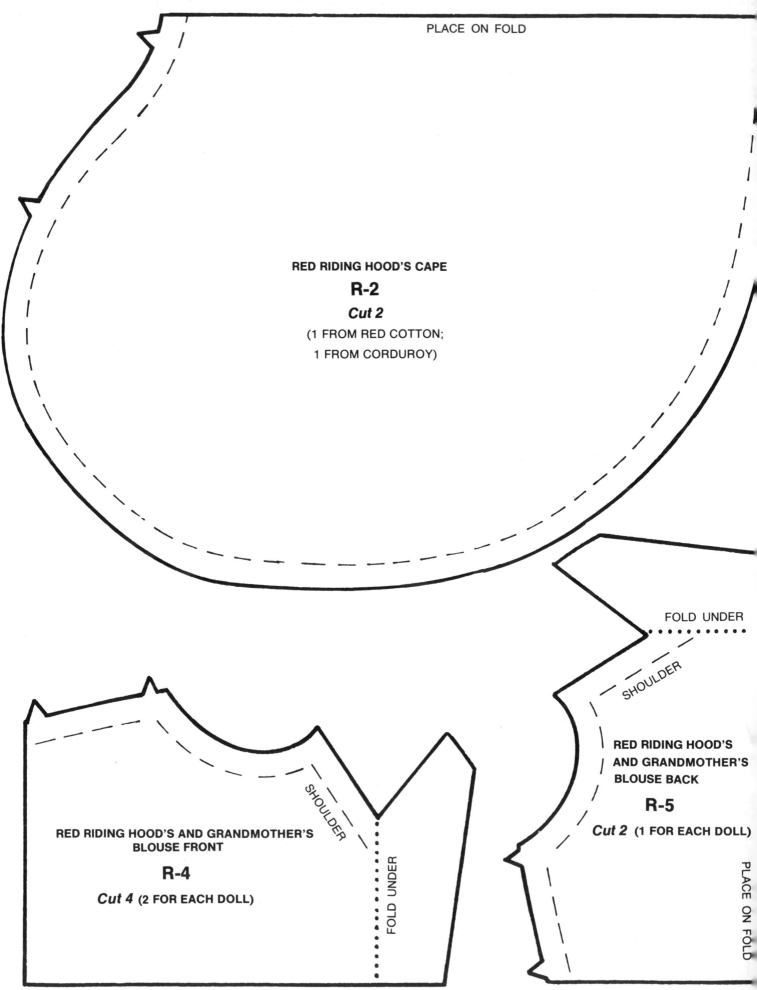

PLACE ON FOLD

RED RIDING HOOD'S CAPE

R-2

Cut 2

(1 FROM RED COTTON;
1 FROM CORDUROY)

FOLD UNDER

SHOULDER

**RED RIDING HOOD'S
AND GRANDMOTHER'S
BLOUSE BACK**

R-5

Cut 2 (1 FOR EACH DOLL)

SHOULDER

FOLD UNDER

**RED RIDING HOOD'S AND GRANDMOTHER'S
BLOUSE FRONT**

R-4

Cut 4 (2 FOR EACH DOLL)

PLACE ON FOLD

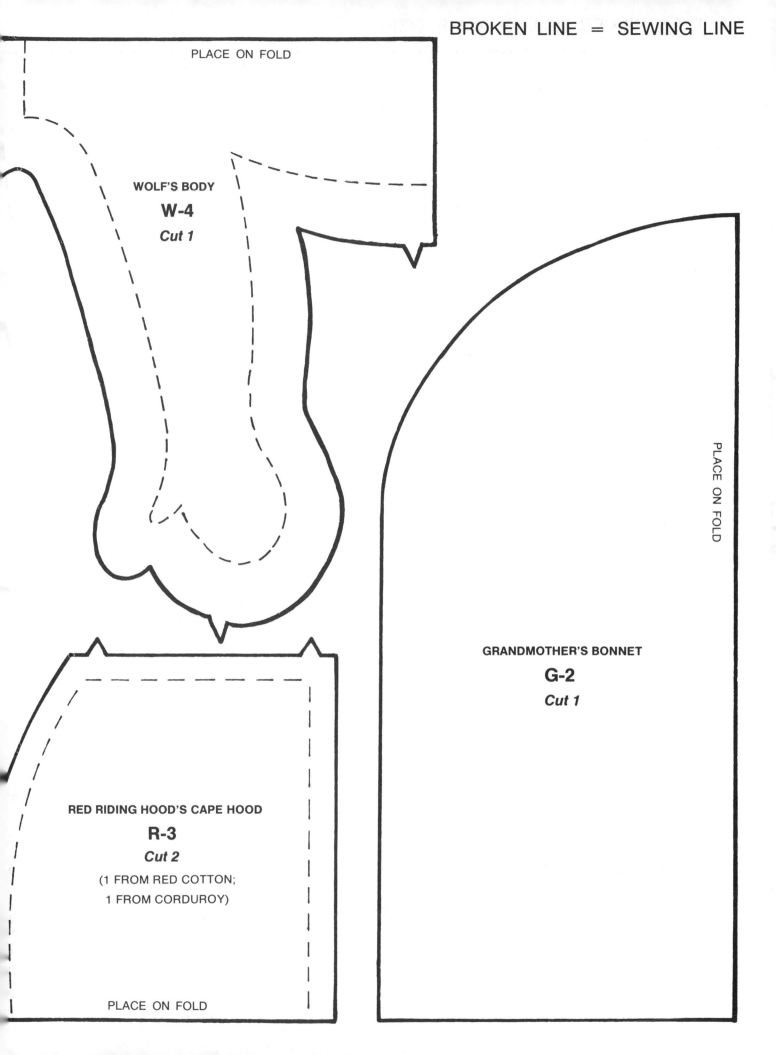

BROKEN LINE = SEWING LINE

PLACE ON FOLD

WOLF'S BODY
W-4
Cut 1

PLACE ON FOLD

GRANDMOTHER'S BONNET
G-2
Cut 1

RED RIDING HOOD'S CAPE HOOD
R-3
Cut 2
(1 FROM RED COTTON;
1 FROM CORDUROY)

PLACE ON FOLD

SEWING AND EMBROIDERY

Red Riding Hood's face:

Using the face drawing (Fig. 1) as a guide, draw Red Riding Hood's face with a pencil onto one of the head-and-body sections. Then, using an embroidery hoop, embroider

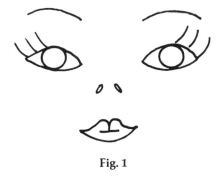

Fig. 1

the features with a single strand of embroidery floss. Use red for the nose and mouth. The nose is done in two small straight stitches worked up and down. The mouth is worked in an outline stitch. Use black for the eyes, eyebrows and eyelashes. The eyes and eyebrows are worked in an outline stitch, the eyelashes in a straight stitch. The iris is blue, worked in a satin stitch.

Red Riding Hood's head-and-body:

Match the notches and baste the head-and-body sections (R-1) together, right sides facing. Machine-stitch where indicated on the pattern, leaving the bottom open for stuffing. Remove basting thread. Trim the seams and clip the curves as illustrated. (Fig. 2). Turn the

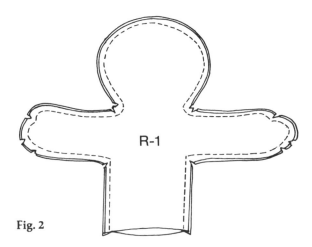

Fig. 2

material right side out and stuff with polyester fiberfill, packing it until the body is very, very stiff. Then hand-stitch the opening with heavy-duty thread, using a whip stitch.

Grandmother's face:

Using the face drawing (Fig. 3) as a guide, draw the grandmother's face with a pencil onto the grandmother's head-and-body section. Then, using an embroidery hoop, em-

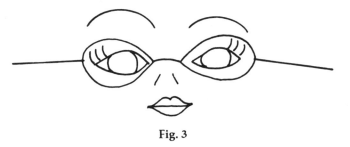

Fig. 3

broider the features with a single strand of embroidery floss. Use red for the nose and mouth. The nose is done in two small straight stitches worked up and down. The mouth is worked in an outline stitch. Use black for the eyes, eyebrows and eyelashes. The eyes and eyebrows are worked in an outline stitch, the eyelashes in a straight stitch. The iris is brown, worked in a satin stitch. Use brown also for the glasses, working in an outline stitch.

Grandmother's and Wolf's head-and-body:

Match the notches and pin and baste the wolf's head sections (W-1, W-2) together. (Fig. 4). Remove pins and machine-stitch.

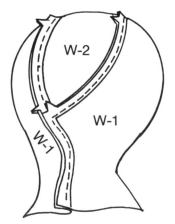

Fig. 4

Remove basting thread. Now baste this piece to the wolf's body section (W-4) at the neck. Machine-stitch and remove basting thread. Set aside.

Baste and machine-stitch two sides of the ears (W-3), right sides facing. Remove basting thread and turn ears right side out. Pin the unstitched side of the ears to the right side of the wolf's head section.

Pin the wolf's completed head-and-body piece to the grandmother's head-and-body section (G-1). Make sure the right sides are facing and that the ears are on the inside. Baste, remove pins and machine-stitch where indicated on the pattern, leaving the bottom open for stuffing. Remove basting thread. Trim the seams and clip the curves. (Fig. 5). Turn the material right side out and push the ears up. The stuffing is done after the wolf's face has been embroidered.

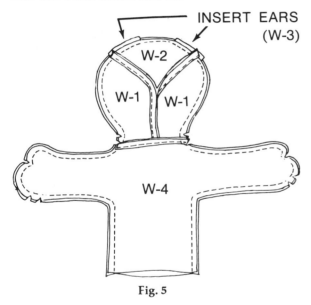

INSERT EARS (W-3)

Fig. 5

Wolf's face:

Using the face drawing (Fig. 6) as a guide, embroider the wolf's features with a single strand of embroidery floss. Use red for the mouth, working in an outline stitch. The nose is worked with black floss in a satin stitch; it should be about ¼" (6 mm.) in diameter. Use black for the eyes and eyebrows, working in an outline stitch. The iris is made with red floss, in three lazy-daisy stitches.

Now stuff with polyester fiberfill, packing it until the body is very, very stiff. Make sure the wolf's nose is *very firm*. Then hand-stitch

Fig. 6

the opening with heavy-duty thread, using a whip stitch.

DOLL ASSEMBLY

When attaching the two parts, turn Red Riding Hood in the same direction as the grandmother. (Fig. 7). Using heavy-duty thread and the whip stitch, hand-stitch Red Riding Hood to the grandmother firmly at the waist so that the doll does not bend.

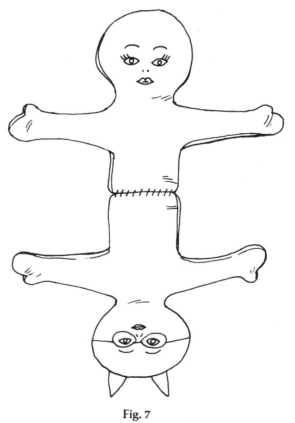

Fig. 7

HAIR

Red Riding Hood:

First make the braids by wrapping yellow yarn 15 times around a 5 x 5″ (12.5 x 12.5 cm.) piece of cardboard. Tie one end with yarn and cut the other end. (Fig. 8). Remove

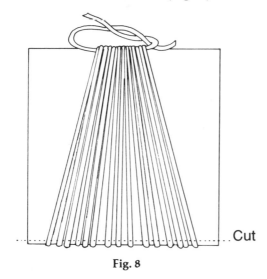

.....Cut

Fig. 8

the cardboard. Thread a needle with the same yarn and stitch the tied end to the head more or less level with the ears, or 1¼″ (3 cm.) from the center back of the head. Divide the yarn into three sections and make the braid, leaving ¾″ (2 cm.) at the bottom, and tie with yarn. (Fig. 9). Trim the ends of the braid. Repeat with the other braid.

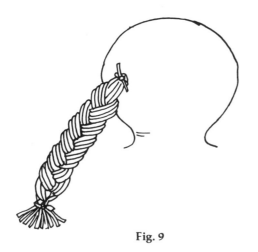

Fig. 9

To make the bangs and the body of the hair, place eight pins across the forehead, ¼″

(6 mm.) above the eyebrows. Place eight more pins across the shoulder 3¾″ (9.5 cm.) from the top head seam. (Fig. 10). Starting with the

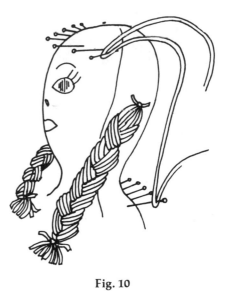

Fig. 10

end pin on the shoulder, bring the yarn around the first pin on the forehead and back to the first pin on the shoulder. Wind the yarn eight times around each pin and use one continuous strand for the entire eight pins.

Thread a needle with the same yarn. Back-stitch across the seam line on the top of the head, starting above the first pin and stitching completely across to above the end pin on the other side of the head. Do the same at the bottom, back-stitching across the bottom of the head about ¾″ (2 cm.) above the pins. Then remove the pins.

Grandmother:

Take three strands of 11″ (27.5 cm.) long gray rug yarn and separate the ply. Place the yarn at the top of the grandmother's head, leaving equal yarn on either side of the head. Use gray thread and stitch the yarn to the grandmother's head at intervals of 1¼″ (3 cm.). Make sure the yarn is a little loose, so that the stitching will make it look like curls. Take the end of the yarn and form small twists on each side of the head and stitch with gray thread. (Fig. 11).

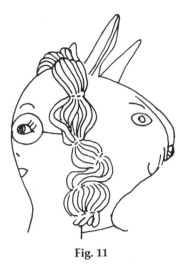

Fig. 11

MAKING THE CLOTHES

Red Riding Hood's cape:

Take the corduroy hood section (R-3) and pin it to the corduroy cape (R-2) at the neck, matching notches. Baste, remove pins and machine-stitch. (Fig. 12). Baste the back of the

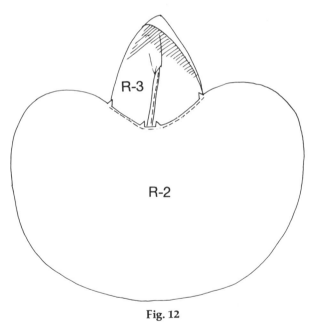

Fig. 12

hood as shown in the illustration and machine-stitch. Remove all basting thread. Do the same with the lining (R-2 and R-3).

Then, with right sides facing, baste and machine-stitch the corduroy and lining together, leaving 2" (5 cm.) open at the bottom of the cape. Remove basting thread and turn cape right side out. Top-stitch around the

cape, but don't top-stitch the hood. Add red ribbons at the neck. Put aside.

Red Riding Hood's blouse:

Baste and machine-stitch the two sections of the front (R-4) to the back (R-5) at the shoulders, right sides facing. Fold under the right side of one blouse front ¼" (6 mm.) and place red lace on top along the folded edge and machine-stitch.

Next, fold under the sleeves (R-6) ¼" (6 mm.) at the cuffs and machine-stitch red lace on them. Set in the sleeves at the armholes and baste them. Then machine-stitch. (Fig. 13). Baste and machine-stitch along the

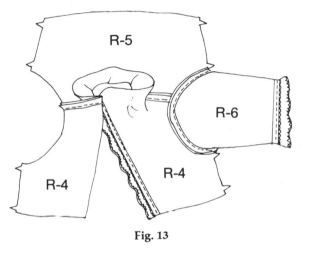

Fig. 13

sleeves and, with notches matching, baste and machine-stitch down the sides. Remove all basting thread. Place the blouse on the doll. Turn under the excess top material at the neck, and hand-stitch the blouse to the doll.

Grandmother's blouse:

Follow the instructions given above for Red Riding Hood's blouse, but use the dark cotton print material and white lace.

Red Riding Hood's and Grandmother's skirts:

The skirts for Red Riding Hood and the grandmother are made together. With right

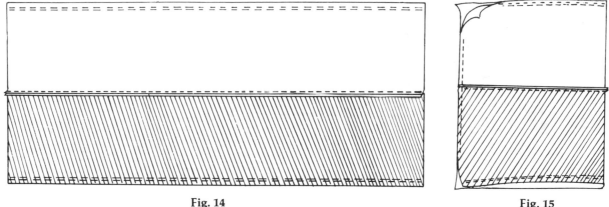

Fig. 14   Fig. 15

sides facing, pin the red cotton material to the dark cotton print material at the hemline, or along the 36″ (90 cm.) edge. Leave a ¼″ (6 mm.) seam and baste it. Remove pins. Machine-stitch the sections together along the hemline. (Fig. 14). Remove basting thread.

Machine-stitch gathering stitches on the other two 36″ (90 cm.) edges, but don't pull to shape as yet. Fold the fabric in half with the right sides facing so that the piece now measures 17½ x 18″ (43.5 x 45 cm.) and baste along the 17½″ (43.5 cm.) edge. (The previously stitched seam now faces itself.) Measure 2″ (5 cm.) in from each end—along basted edge—and mark with pins. (Fig. 15). Next machine-stitch between these pin marks, back-stitching at the beginning and end to secure the seam. Remove pins and basting thread.

Now turn this tubular piece inside out, wrong sides facing, and match the top raw edges as shown in illustration. (Fig. 16). Top-stitch along the hemline. The raw edges become the skirt waistlines. The seams become the center backs of the skirts.

Red Riding Hood's and Grandmother's waistbands:

With right sides facing, fold the red cotton print waistband strip—10 x 1¾″ (25 x 4.5 cm.)—in half lengthwise and machine-stitch each end. Back-stitch to make them secure. Next, turn the piece to the right side and press. Pull to shape the top raw edge of the red print skirt to fit the waistband. Turn

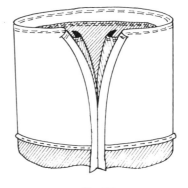

Fig. 16

under one right side raw edge of the band and pin to the right side top raw edge of the red cotton skirt, matching each end with the center-back seam of the skirt. Baste, remove pins and machine-stitch. Remove basting thread.

Flip the waistband over the top of the skirt and, turning under the remaining raw edge of the band, hemstitch it to the other side to encase the top raw edge of the same skirt. (Fig. 17). Repeat this procedure with the dark

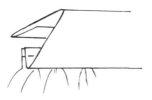

Fig. 17

cotton print waistband to encase the top raw edge of the dark cotton print skirt at the waist. Put aside.

Grandmother's bonnet:

Turn under the entire edge ¼" (6 mm.), baste and hem. Remove basting thread. Then machine-stitch white lace all around except the straight edge. Gather the bonnet by hand-stitching elastic thread near the lace, starting ⅝" (1.5 cm.) from the bottom. Then gather across the straight edge, again ⅝" (1.5 cm.) from the bottom. Stitch white ribbons ½" (1.25 cm.) from the bottom on both sides. Place the bonnet on the grandmother's head, covering the wolf's face. The bonnet can be pulled down to show the wolf's face.

Grandmother's apron:

Hem the white cotton material ¼" (6 mm.) on all sides and machine-stitch the white ribbon across one 3" (7.5 cm.) side to make the apron. Put aside.

FINISHING

Put the red skirt on Red Riding Hood. The seam should be at the back. Hand-stitch the waistband to the doll and hand-stitch the skirt's seam closed. Turn the doll upside down and hand-stitch the other waistband to the grandmother. Hand-stitch the skirt's seam closed. Tie the apron around the grandmother's waist. Turn the doll back to Red Riding Hood's side and tie the cape hood around Red Riding Hood's neck.

Mary and the Little Lamb

MARY HAD A *little lamb,*
Its fleece was white as snow;
And everywhere that Mary went
The lamb was sure to go.

Mary and the Little Lamb

MATERIALS YOU'LL NEED

¼ yard (22.5 cm.) light pink cotton material—Mary's head-and-body (M-1, M-2)

½ yard (45 cm.) white terry cloth—lamb's head-and-body (L-1 through L-4)

¼ yard (22.5 cm.) white cotton material—lamb's muzzle (L-5, L-6)

A scrap of pink felt—lamb's tongue

A scrap of black felt—lamb's hoofs, eyes (L-7, L-8)

¾ yard (67.5 cm.) print (small design) cotton material—Mary's bonnet, blouse, skirt (M-3 through M-7)

1 yard (90 cm.) solid color material to match print—Mary's pinafore (M-8, M-9) and lamb's skirt

1-ounce skein of yellow baby yarn—Mary's hair

1 yard (90 cm.) of narrow ribbon—Mary's hair and pinafore

1½ yards (135 cm.) medium-width lace—Mary's bonnet

Black, red, blue, and white embroidery floss for faces

1 small book—under Mary's arm

Sewing thread and heavy-duty thread to match materials

1½ pounds of polyester fiberfill for stuffing

Note: All seam allowances are ½'' (1.25 cm.) for dolls, and ¼'' (6 mm.) for clothes.

CUTTING

Mary's head-and-body and clothes:

Make the paper patterns from the pattern pieces (M-1 through M-9), enlarging, if needed, to actual size. Cut all pattern pieces from material, remembering to reverse the pattern when pairs are needed. The cuffs (M-7) should be cut on the bias.

For Mary's skirt, cut a rectangle 36 x 12'' (90 x 30 cm.), and a strip 11 x 1¾'' (27.5 x 4.5 cm.) for the waistband.

For Mary's blouse, cut a strip 3½ x ½'' (8.75 x 1.25 cm.) from the cotton print material.

For Mary's pinafore skirt, cut a rectangle 26 x 10'' (65 x 25 cm.).

Lamb's head-and-body and clothes:

Make the paper patterns from the pattern pieces (L-1 through L-8), enlarging, if needed, to actual size. Cut all pattern pieces from material, remembering to reverse the pattern when pairs are needed.

For the lamb's skirt, cut a rectangle 36 x 12'' (90 x 30 cm.), and a strip 11 x 1 ¾'' (27.5 x 4.5 cm.) for the waistband.

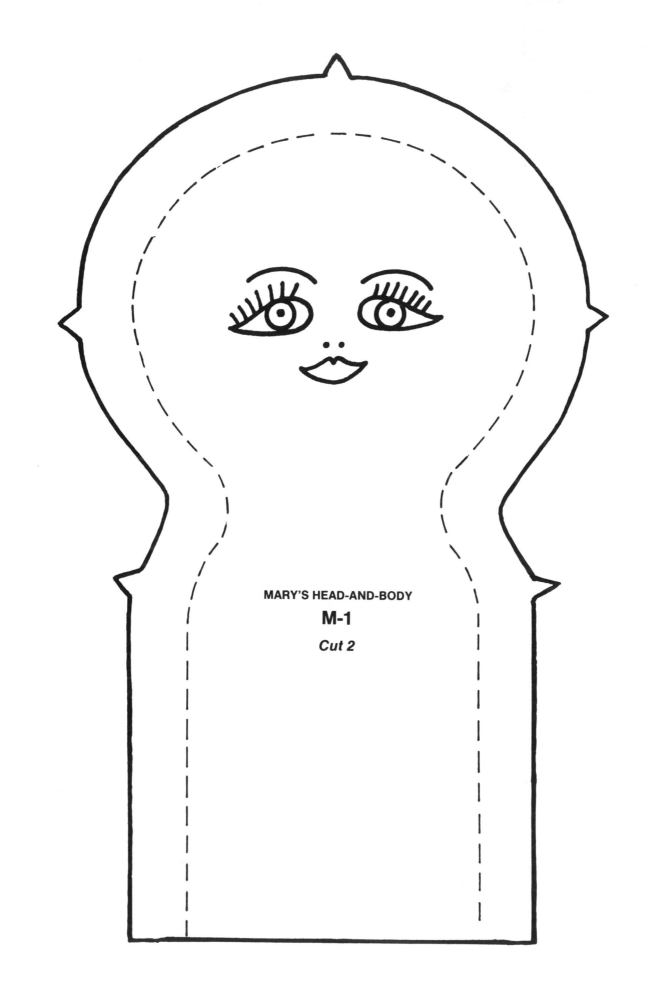

MARY'S HEAD-AND-BODY

M-1

Cut 2

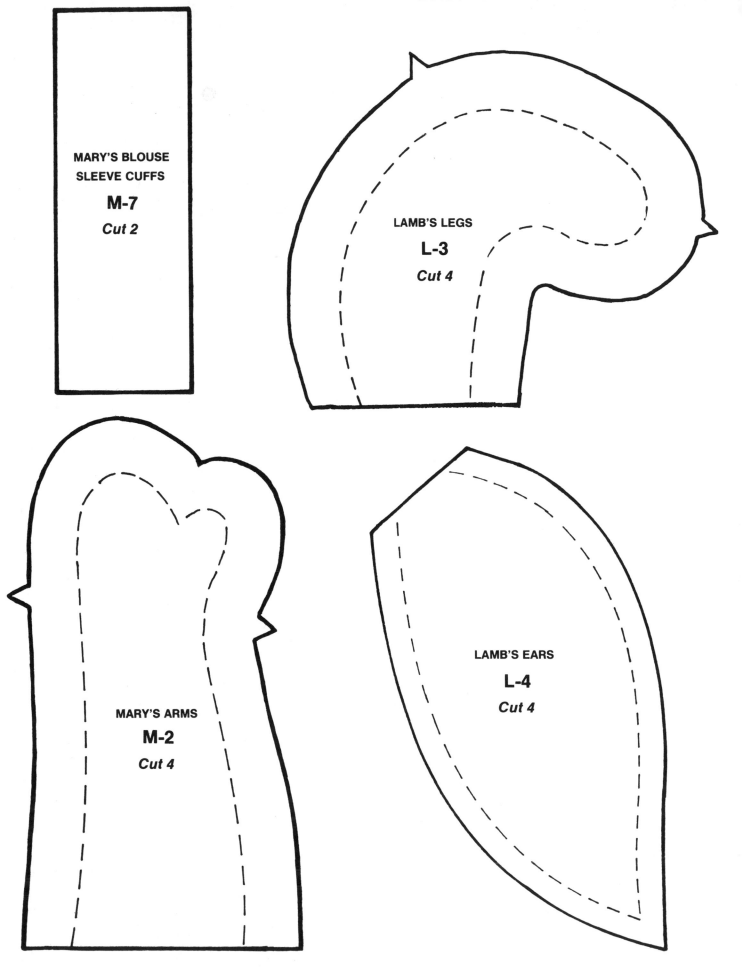

BROKEN LINE = SEWING LINE

MARY'S BLOUSE
SLEEVE CUFFS
M-7
Cut 2

LAMB'S LEGS
L-3
Cut 4

MARY'S ARMS
M-2
Cut 4

LAMB'S EARS
L-4
Cut 4

PATTERN PIECES DRAWN SAME SIZE

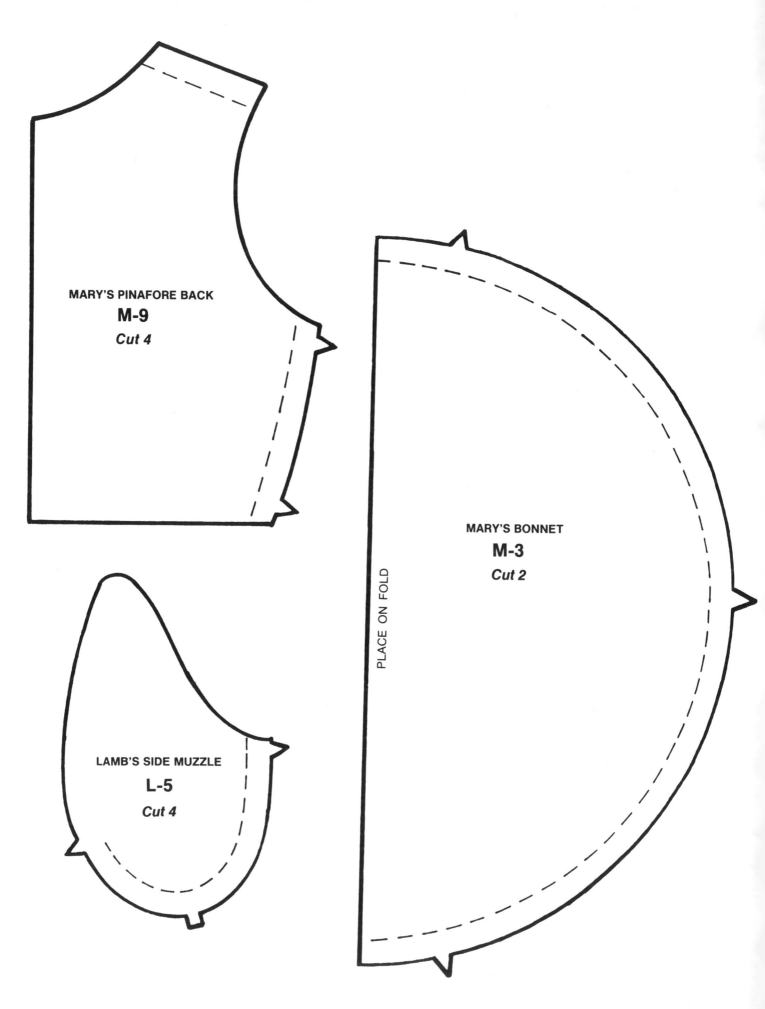

MARY'S PINAFORE BACK
M-9
Cut 4

MARY'S BONNET
M-3
Cut 2

PLACE ON FOLD

LAMB'S SIDE MUZZLE
L-5
Cut 4

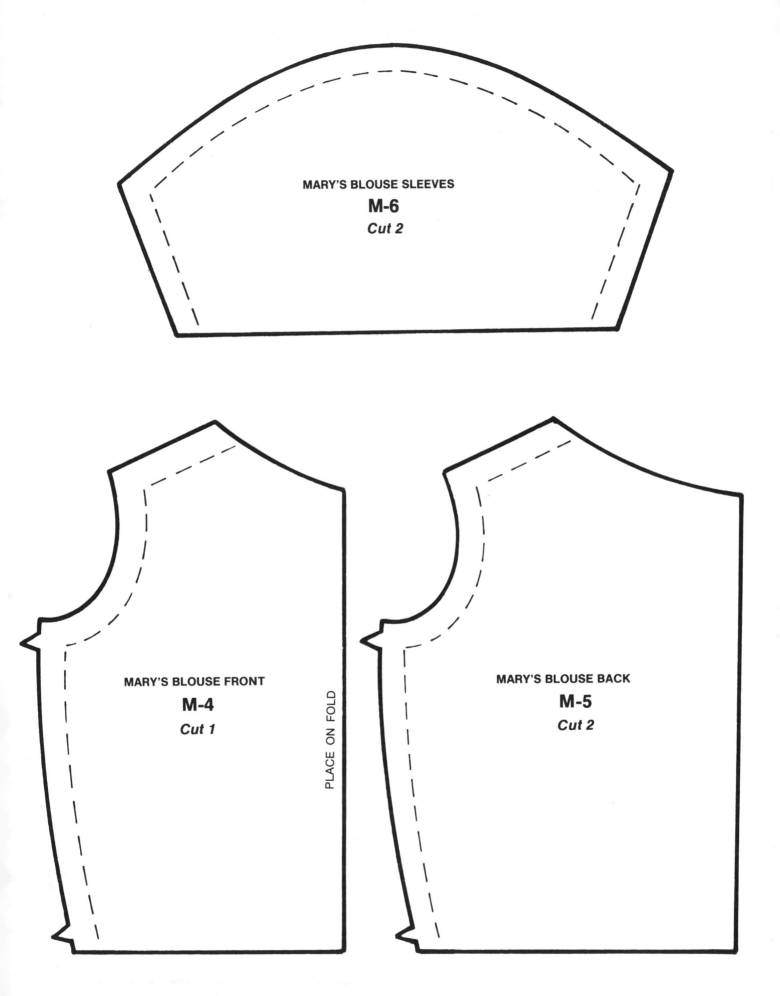

BROKEN LINE = SEWING LINE

MARY'S BLOUSE SLEEVES
M-6
Cut 2

MARY'S BLOUSE FRONT
M-4
Cut 1

PLACE ON FOLD

MARY'S BLOUSE BACK
M-5
Cut 2

PATTERN PIECES DRAWN SAME SIZE

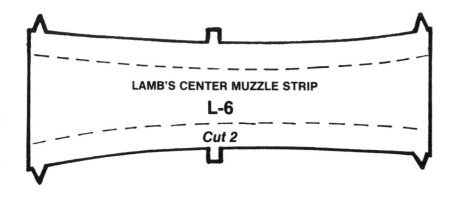

LAMB'S CENTER MUZZLE STRIP

L-6

Cut 2

L-7

LAMB'S HOOFS

Cut 2

LAMB'S EYES

L-8

Cut 2

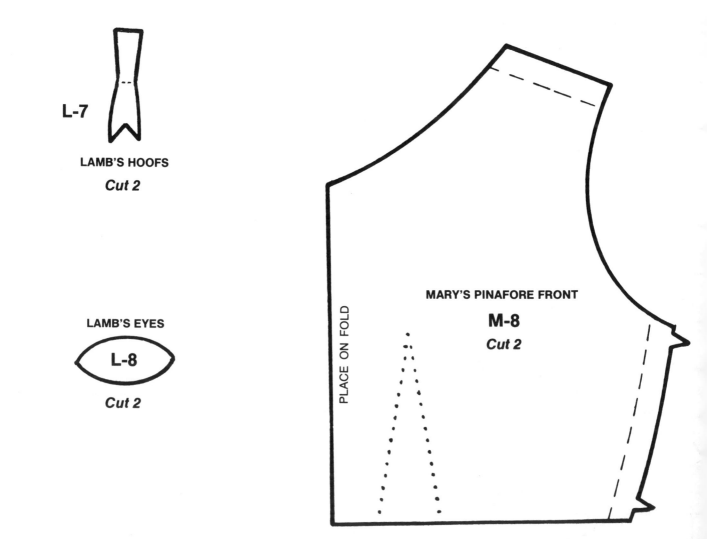

MARY'S PINAFORE FRONT

M-8

Cut 2

PLACE ON FOLD

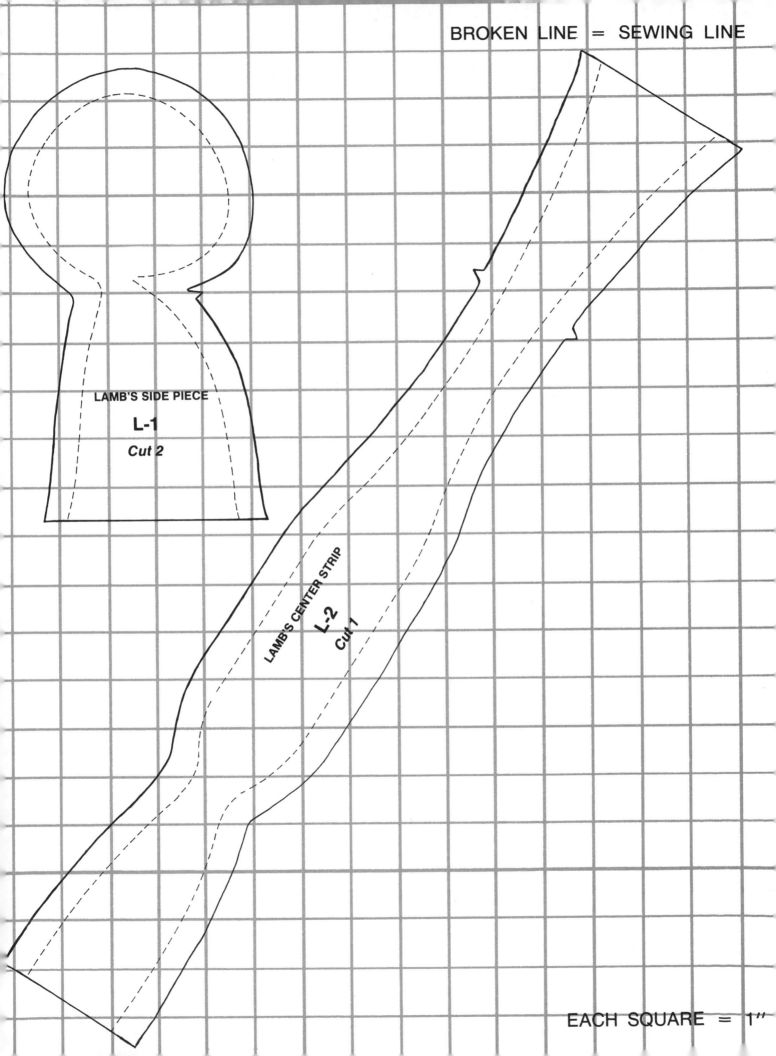

BROKEN LINE = SEWING LINE

LAMB'S SIDE PIECE

L-1

Cut 2

LAMB'S CENTER STRIP

L-2

Cut 1

EACH SQUARE = 1"

SEWING AND EMBROIDERING

Mary's face:

Using the face drawing (Fig. 1) as a guide, draw Mary's face with a pencil onto one of the head-and-body sections. Then, using an embroidery hoop, embroider the features with a single strand of embroidery floss. Use red for the nose and mouth, working in an outline stitch. Use black for the eyes and eyebrows, again working in an outline stitch. Use black for the eyelashes, also, but work in a straight stitch. Use blue for the iris and work in a buttonhole stitch. The pupil is black and worked in a French knot.

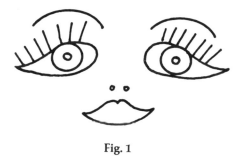

Fig. 1

Mary's head-and-body:

Match the notches and baste the head-and-body sections (M-1) together, right sides facing. Machine-stitch where indicated on the pattern, leaving the bottom open for stuffing. Remove basting thread. Trim the seams and clip the neck curves as illustrated. (Fig. 2).

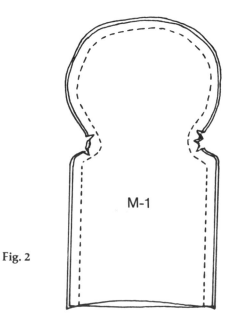

Fig. 2

Turn the material right side out and stuff with polyester fiberfill, packing it until the body is very, very stiff. Then hand-stitch the opening with heavy-duty thread, using a whip stitch.

Mary's arms:

Match the notches and baste two arm sections (M-2) together, right sides facing. Machine-stitch where indicated on the pattern, leaving the bottom open for stuffing. Remove basting thread. Trim the seams and clip the corners. (Fig. 3). Repeat with the

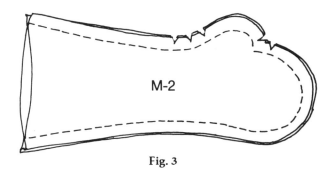

Fig. 3

other arm. Turn the material right side out and stuff as above. Turn in the opening and whip-stitch the arms to the body with heavy-duty thread. (Fig. 4).

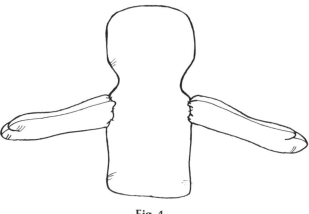

Fig. 4

Lamb's head-and-body:

Take one of the lamb's side pieces (L-1) and ease the lamb's center strip (L-2) around it. (Fig. 5). Pin and baste these together. Make

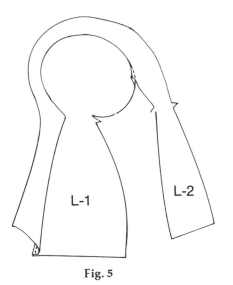

Fig. 5

sure the notch on the side piece matches with the notch on the center strip. Then remove pins and machine-stitch. Add the second side piece to the other side of the center strip in the same way.

Trim the seams and clip the curves. Remove basting thread. Turn the material right side out and stuff with polyester fiberfill, packing it until the body is very, very stiff. Then hand-stitch the opening with heavy-duty thread, using a whip stitch.

Lamb's feet:

Insert one hoof (L-7) between the leg sections (L-3) as shown in illustration. (Fig. 6). Pin and baste all around, leaving the straight edge open for stuffing. Then remove pins,

and machine-stitch, making sure the hoof has been stitched in. Remove basting thread. Trim the seams and clip the curves.

Then turn the material right side out and stuff with polyester fiberfill, packing it until the leg is very, very stiff. Repeat with the other leg. Finally, position both legs (Fig. 7) and hand-stitch to the body with the heavy duty thread, using a whip stitch.

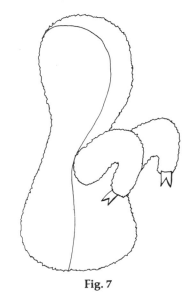

Fig. 7

Lamb's muzzle:

Fold back one center muzzle strip (L-6) ¼" (6 mm.). The fold-back should be just below the square notches. Then cut the tongue from pink felt and position it as shown in illustration. (Fig. 8). Baste and machine-stitch across the fold-back. Make sure the tongue has been stitched in.

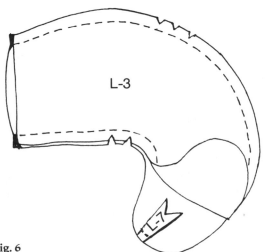

Fig. 6

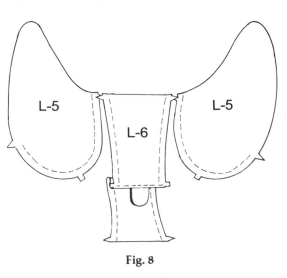

Fig. 8

Next, pin and baste two side muzzle sections (L-5) to the center strip, one on each side, as far as the triangular notches. (See Fig. 8.) Make sure that all the notches match. Now, remove pins, and machine-stitch where basted. Remove basting thread. Trim the edges and clip the curves.

Repeat this procedure with the other center muzzle strip and side muzzle sections, but don't add a tongue. Now match these two muzzle pieces and, with right sides facing, baste and machine-stitch, leaving an opening for turning. Turn material right side out and stitch the opening closed.

Stuff the double muzzle lightly with polyester fiberfill, i.e., put the stuffing behind both muzzles, not in between. Now fit this over the snout of the lamb, and hand-stitch all around to secure. Next, mark the position of the nose and mouth, using the illustration (Fig. 9) as a guide. Embroider the facial details on the muzzle with two strands of black embroidery floss.

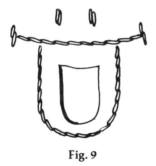

Fig. 9

Lamb's ears:

Baste two ear sections (L-4) together and machine-stitch where indicated on the pattern. Remove basting thread. Trim the seams and clip the curves. (Fig. 10). Repeat with the

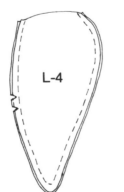

L-4

Fig. 10

other ear. Then turn the material right side out, turn under the raw edges, and hand-stitch the ears in line with the top seam of the lamb's head. (Fig. 11). Also hand-stitch ½" (1.25 cm.) down each side to keep the ears in place.

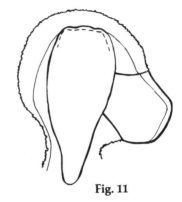

Fig. 11

Lamb's eyes:

Embroider the eyes (L-8) with white floss, working in a cross stitch. (Fig. 12). Then topstitch the eyes in place.

Fig. 12

DOLL ASSEMBLY

When attaching the two parts together, turn Mary in the opposite direction from the lamb. (Fig. 13). Using heavy-duty thread and the whip stitch, hand-stitch Mary to the lamb firmly at the waist so that the doll does not bend.

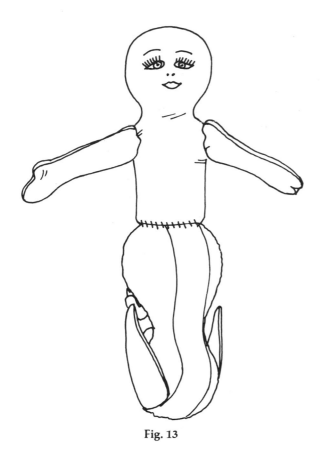

Fig. 13

HAIR

Mary:

Make the bangs by looping yellow yarn 15 times around a 3 x 1½" (7.5 x 3.75 cm.) piece of cardboard. Use the 1½"(3.75 cm.) side for looping. (Fig. 14). Then remove the

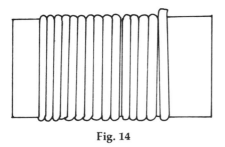

Fig. 14

cardboard and hand-stitch the bangs to the head. (Fig. 15).

Loop some more yellow yarn 130 times around a 12 x 12" (30 x 30 cm.) piece of cardboard. Remove the cardboard and ma-

Fig. 15

chine-stitch down the center to secure the yarn and form a part. The yarn should now be 6" (15 cm.) on either side of the part. Cut across the loops.

Hand-stitch the center of the yarn (along the part) to the top of Mary's head, from the forehead to the nape of the neck. Frame the yarn around the face. Hand-stitch the yarn at intervals to secure. Make the braids, secure them with thread and then tie ribbons. (Fig. 16). Stitch the braids to the face at the point where the neck starts, so that the braids stay in front.

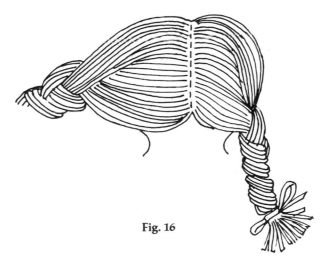

Fig. 16

MAKING THE CLOTHES

Mary's bonnet:

Take the two sections of the bonnet (M-3) and, with right sides facing, match the notches. Now insert lace between these two pieces; the outer edge of the lace should be in line with the edge of the bonnet. Baste and machine-stitch as marked on the pattern, leaving an opening for turning. Remove basting thread and turn material right side out. Hand-stitch the opening closed.

Next, machine-stitch two rows of gathering stitches 1″ (2.5 cm.) from the edge of the bonnet, i.e., the edge of the cotton material, not the lace. Pull to shape and knot the thread to secure. (Fig. 17). Stitch the bonnet onto Mary's head.

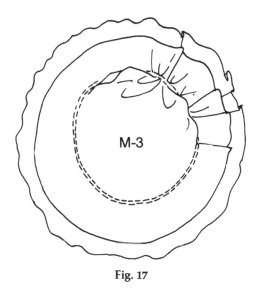

Fig. 17

Mary's blouse:

First take the 3½ x ½″ (8.75 x 1.25 cm.) strip and fold under the raw edges. Place this strip in the center of the blouse front (M-4), and insert lace on either side of the strip. The

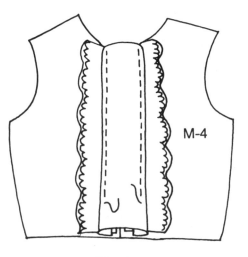

Fig. 18

lace should be a little under the strip so it can be stitched in. Baste and machine-stitch down both edges of the strip. (Fig. 18).

Now, baste and machine-stitch the two sections of the back (M-5) to the front at the shoulders, right sides facing. Then cut a band on the bias from the same print material to fit the neck. The band should be about ¾″ (3.75 cm.) wide. Fold this band in half lengthwise, turn under the raw edges and encase the neck of the blouse in this band. Baste and top-stitch. (Fig. 19).

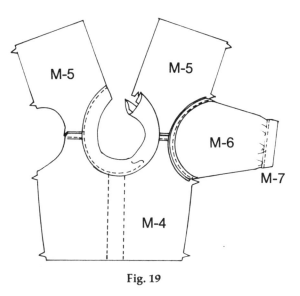

Fig. 19

Next, take the sleeves (M-6) and gather the straight edge a little to fit the cuffs (M-7). Fold the cuffs in half lengthwise, turn under the raw edges and encase the sleeve edge. Baste and top-stitch. Set the sleeves in the armholes of the blouse, baste and machine-stitch. Then baste and machine-stitch down the sides of the sleeves.

Match the notches of the front with those of the back sections, baste and machine-stitch down the sides. Remove all basting thread. Fit the blouse on the doll, turn under one raw edge of the back, place it over the other and hemstitch it closed.

Mary's and Lamb's skirts:

The skirts for Mary and the lamb are made together. With right sides facing, pin

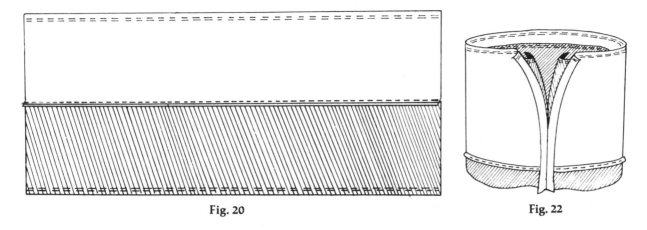

Fig. 20

the print cotton material to the solid color cotton material at the hemline, or along the 36" (90 cm.) edge. Leave a ¼" (6 mm.) seam and baste it. Remove pins. Machine-stitch the sections together along the hemline. (Fig. 20). Remove basting thread.

Machine-stitch gathering stitches on the other two 36" (90 cm.) edges, but don't pull the shape as yet. Fold the fabric in half with the right sides facing so that the piece now measures 23½ x 18" (58.75 x 45 cm.) and baste along the 23½" (58.75 cm.) edge. (The previously stitched seam now faces itself.) Measure 2" (5 cm.) in from each end—along basted edge—and mark with pins. (Fig. 21).

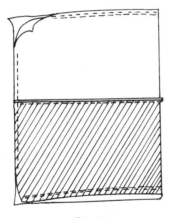

Fig. 21

Next, machine-stitch between these pin marks, back-stitching at the beginning and end to secure the seam. Remove pins and basting thread.

Now turn this tubular piece inside out, wrong sides facing, and match the top raw edges as shown in illustration. (Fig. 22). Top-

stitch along the hemline. The raw edges become the skirt waistlines. The seams become the center backs of the skirts.

Mary's and Lamb's waistbands:

With right sides facing, fold the print waistband strip—11 x 1¾" (27.5 x 4.5 cm.)—in half lengthwise and machine-stitch each end. Back-stitch to make them secure. Next, turn the piece to the right side and press. Pull to shape the top raw edge of the print skirt to fit the waistband. Turn under one right side raw edge of the band and pin to the right side top raw edge of the print skirt, matching each end with the center-back seam of the skirt. Baste, remove pins, and machine-stitch. Remove basting thread.

Flip the waistband over the top of the skirt and, turning under the remaining raw edge of the band, hemstitch it to the other side to encase the top raw edge of the same skirt. (Fig. 23). Repeat this procedure with the solid color waistband to encase the top raw edge of the solid color skirt at the waist.

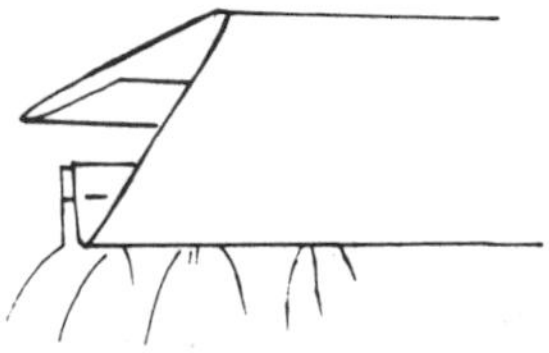

Fig. 22

Fig. 23

Mary's pinafore top:

(The pinafore top is made with a lining from the same material.) First, sew the darts on the two sections of the front (M-8) where indicated on the pattern. Then, with right sides facing, baste and machine-stitch these two pieces around the neck and arms. Clip the curves. Now, take two back sections (M-9) and baste and machine-stitch them also at the neck and arms. Clip the curves. Repeat with the other two back sections. Remove all basting thread and turn both the front and back pieces right side out. Baste and machine-stitch the front to the back pieces at the shoulders and sides. Remove basting thread.

Mary's pinafore skirt:

Take the 26 x 10 " (65 x 25 cm.) pieces and hem the 10" (25 cm.) sides ¼" (6 mm.). Hem the bottom—one 26" (65 cm.) side—1" (2.5 cm.). Machine-stitch two rows of gathering stitches on the other 26" (65 cm.) side and pull to shape so that it fits the pinafore top. Baste and machine-stitch the skirt to the top. Remove basting thread. Add ribbons at the waistline and to the back pieces of the top. (Fig. 24).

FINISHING

Put the skirt on Mary. The seam should be on one side. Hand-stitch the waistband to the doll and hand-stitch the skirt's side seam closed. Turn the doll upside down and hand-stitch the other waistband to the lamb. Hand-stitch the skirt's side seam closed. Turn the doll back to Mary's side and place the pinafore on her. Tie the ribbons on top and at the waist. Tape the small book under Mary's right arm and hand-stitch the pinafore skirt to Mary's right hand.

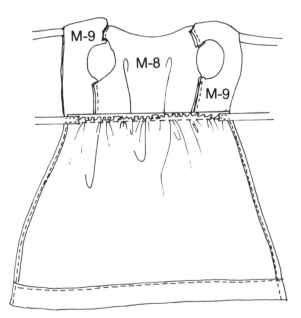

Fig. 24

Goldilocks and the Three Bears

Once upon a time *there were three gentle bears who lived together in a tidy house in the deep woods. . . . One day while the bears were out, a little girl called Goldilocks happened to find their house. . . .*

Goldilocks and the Three Bears

MATERIALS YOU'LL NEED

¼ yard (22.5 cm.) light pink cotton material—Goldilocks' head-and-body (G-1)

¾ yard (67.5 cm.) brown cotton material—bears' heads-and-bodies (B-1 through B-12)

A scrap of white felt—bears' eyes (B-19)

A scrap of black felt—bears' eyes (iris) (B-19)

½ yard (45 cm.) print cotton material—Goldilocks' blouse and skirt (G-2, G-3, G-4)

⅓ yard (30 cm.) solid color cotton material—bears' skirt, Mama Bear's bib and straps (B-17, B-18)

A 9 x 12″ (22.5 x 30 cm.) piece of felt to match—bears' vests and bow ties (B-13 through B-16)

A 6 x 6″ (15 x 15 cm.) piece of white cotton material—bears' dickeys

4-ounce skein of yellow baby yarn—Goldilocks' hair

1 yard (90 cm.) medium-width lace—Goldilocks' blouse

2 small white buttons—bears' vests

Black, red, and blue embroidery floss for faces

Sewing thread and heavy-duty thread to match materials

1½ pounds of polyester fiberfill for stuffing

Note: All seam allowances are ½″ (1.25 cm.) for dolls, and ¼″ (6 mm.) for clothes.

CUTTING

Goldilocks' head-and-body and clothes:

Make the paper patterns from the pattern pieces (G-1 through G-4), enlarging, if needed, to actual size. Cut all pattern pieces from material, remembering to reverse the pattern when pairs are needed.

For Goldilocks' skirt, cut a rectangle 27 x 9″ (67.5 x 22.5 cm.), and a strip 11 x 1¾″ (27.5 x 4.5 cm.) for the waistband.

Bears' heads-and-bodies and clothes:

Make the paper patterns from the pattern pieces (B-1 through B-19), enlarging, if needed, to actual size. Cut all pattern pieces from material, remembering to reverse the pattern when pairs are needed.

For the bears' skirt, cut a rectangle 27 x 9″ (67.5 x 22.5 cm.), and a strip 11 x 1¾″ (27.5 x 4.5 cm.) for the waistband.

For the dickeys, cut a piece 4 x 2½″ (10 x 6.25 cm.) from white cotton material for Papa Bear, and another piece 3 x 2″ (7.5 x 5 cm.) for Baby Bear. Cut two bow ties from matching pieces of felt, 1 x ½″ (2.5 x 1.25 cm.), and ¾ x ¼″ (2 cm. x 6 mm.). The larger one is for Papa Bear, the smaller one is for Baby Bear.

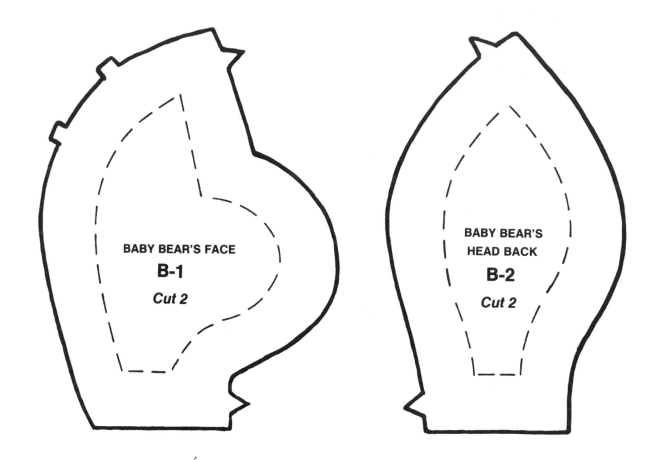

BABY BEAR'S FACE
B-1
Cut 2

BABY BEAR'S
HEAD BACK
B-2
Cut 2

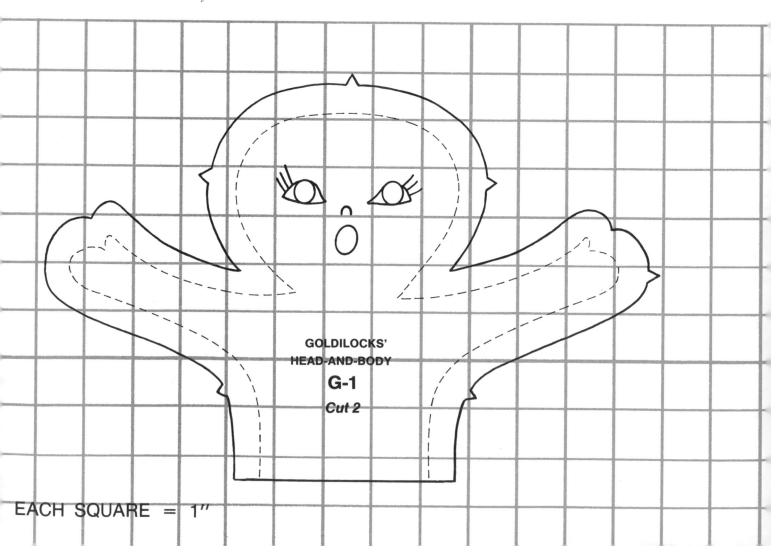

GOLDILOCKS'
HEAD-AND-BODY
G-1
Cut 2

EACH SQUARE = 1"

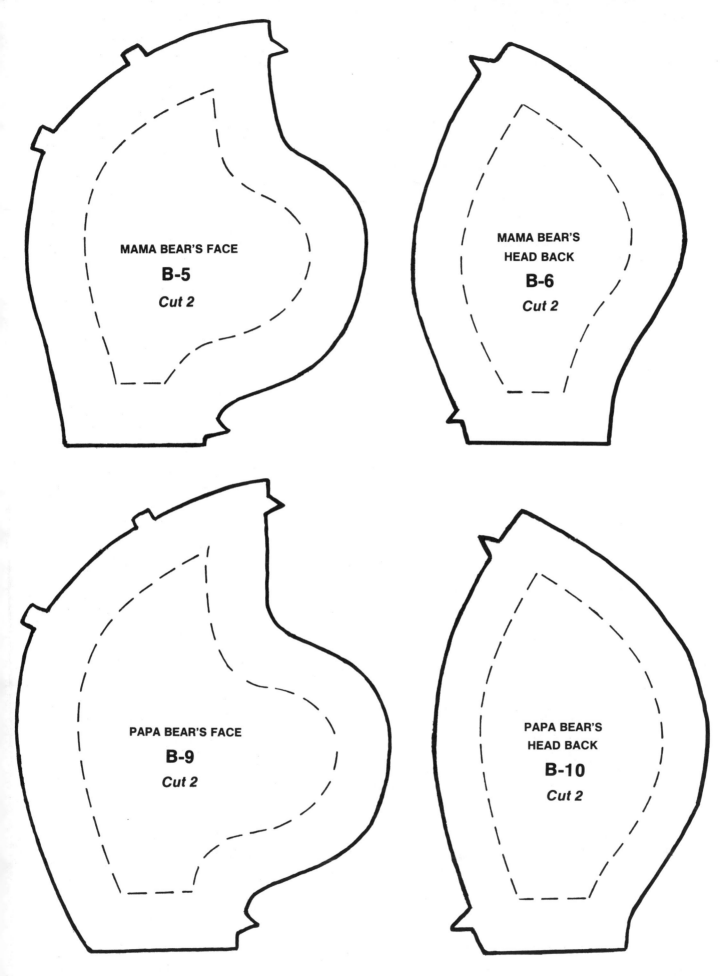

BROKEN LINE = SEWING LINE

MAMA BEAR'S FACE

B-5

Cut 2

MAMA BEAR'S
HEAD BACK

B-6

Cut 2

PAPA BEAR'S FACE

B-9

Cut 2

PAPA BEAR'S
HEAD BACK

B-10

Cut 2

PATTERN PIECES DRAWN SAME SIZE

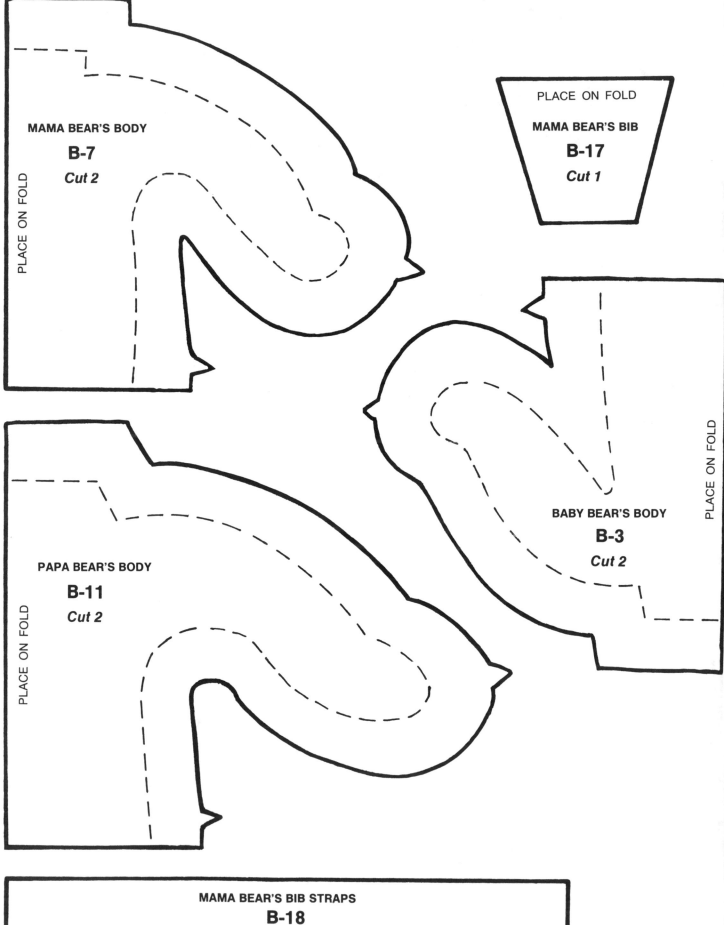

MAMA BEAR'S BODY

B-7

Cut 2

PLACE ON FOLD

PLACE ON FOLD

MAMA BEAR'S BIB

B-17

Cut 1

PAPA BEAR'S BODY

B-11

Cut 2

PLACE ON FOLD

BABY BEAR'S BODY

B-3

Cut 2

PLACE ON FOLD

MAMA BEAR'S BIB STRAPS

B-18

Cut 2

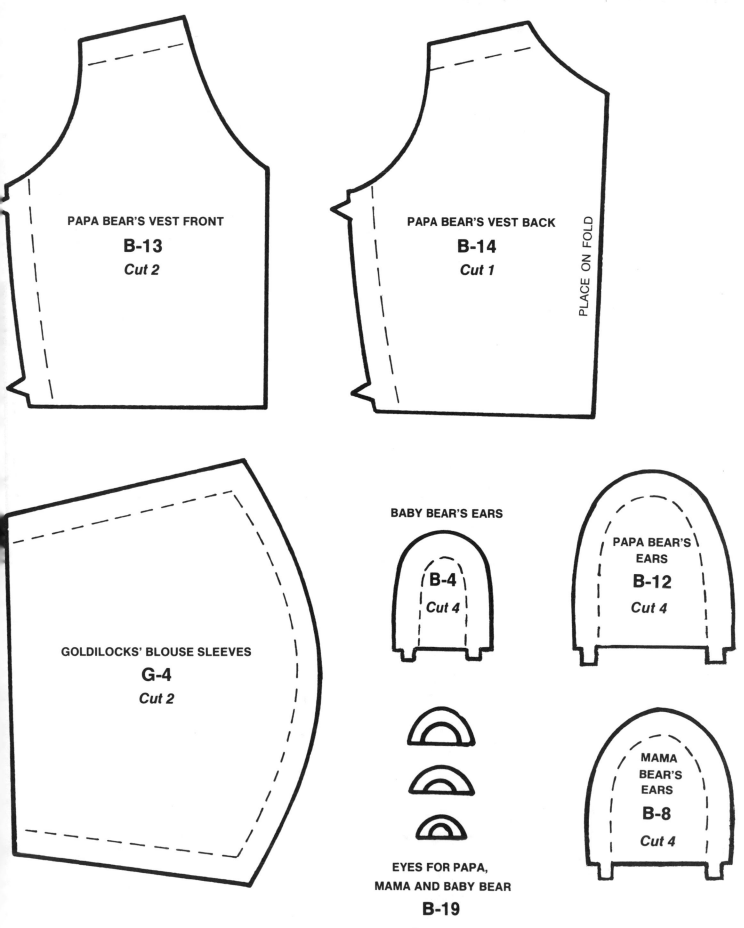

BROKEN LINE = SEWING LINE

PAPA BEAR'S VEST FRONT

B-13

Cut 2

PAPA BEAR'S VEST BACK

B-14

Cut 1

PLACE ON FOLD

GOLDILOCKS' BLOUSE SLEEVES

G-4

Cut 2

BABY BEAR'S EARS

B-4

Cut 4

PAPA BEAR'S
EARS

B-12

Cut 4

MAMA
BEAR'S
EARS

B-8

Cut 4

EYES FOR PAPA,
MAMA AND BABY BEAR

B-19

Cut 2 each

PATTERN PIECES DRAWN SAME SIZE
BROKEN LINE = SEWING LINE

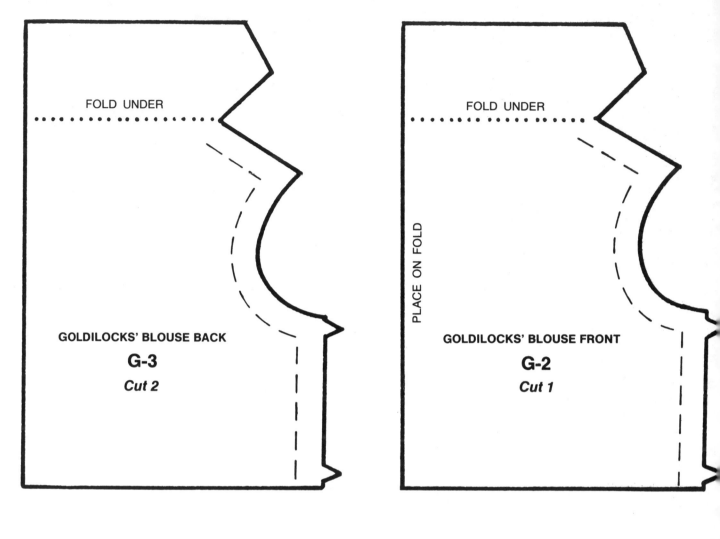

FOLD UNDER

GOLDILOCKS' BLOUSE BACK

G-3

Cut 2

FOLD UNDER

PLACE ON FOLD

GOLDILOCKS' BLOUSE FRONT

G-2

Cut 1

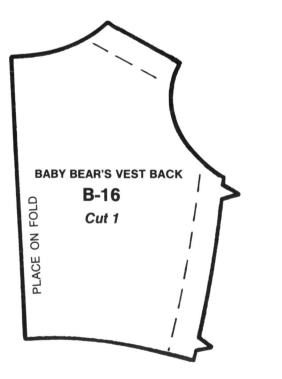

BABY BEAR'S VEST BACK

B-16

Cut 1

PLACE ON FOLD

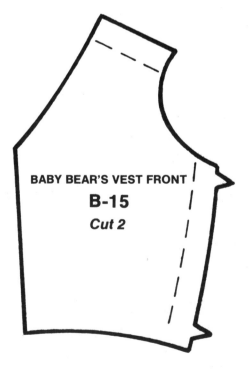

BABY BEAR'S VEST FRONT

B-15

Cut 2

SEWING AND EMBROIDERING

Goldilocks' face:

Using the face drawing (Fig. 1) as a guide, draw Goldilocks' face with a pencil onto one of the head-and-body sections. Then, using an embroidery hoop, embroider the features with a single strand of embroidery floss. Use

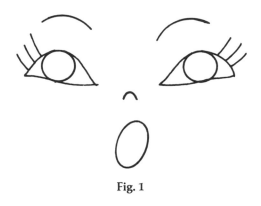

Fig. 1

red for the nose and mouth, working in an outline stitch. Use black for the eyes, eyebrows and eyelashes, with the eyes and eyebrows worked in an outline stitch and the eyelashes in a straight stitch. The iris is blue, worked in a satin stitch. The pupil is black and worked in a French knot.

Goldilocks' head-and-body:

Match the notches and baste the head-and-body sections (G-1) together, right sides facing. Machine-stitch where indicated on the pattern, leaving the bottom open for stuffing. Remove basting thread. Trim the seams and clip the curves as illustrated. (Fig. 2). Turn the

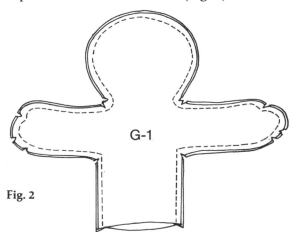

Fig. 2

material right side out and stuff with polyester fiberfill, packing it until the body is very, very stiff. Then hand-stitch the opening with heavy-duty thread, using a whip stitch.

Bears' heads-and-bodies:

Baby Bear is made first. Take the two face sections (B-1), match the triangular notches and pin down that side only. Baste, remove pins and machine-stitch. Then baste this face piece to one body section (B-3) at the neck. Machine-stitch. Next, take the two sections of the head back (B-2), and again matching the triangular notches, pin down that side only. Baste, remove pins and machine-stitch. Then baste this head-back piece to the second body section (B-3).

Now, for the ears, baste and machine-stitch two ear sections (B-4) as marked on the pattern, with right sides facing. Remove basting thread and clip the curves. Turn ear right side out. Do the same with the other ear. Then pin these ears to the right side of the bear's face (B-1). The square notches of the ears should match the square notches of the face. Make sure the ears are pointing downwards. Baste, remove pins and machine-stitch. (Fig. 3).

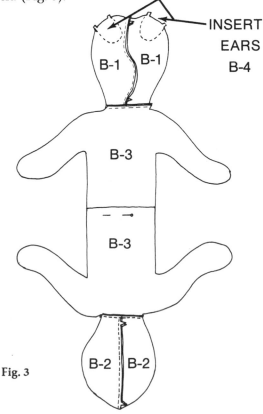

Fig. 3

Now put the two head-and-body pieces together, right sides facing. Baste and machine-stitch, leaving the bottom open for stuffing. Remove all basting thread. Trim the seams and clip the curves. Turn material right side out. Stuff everything, *except the ears,* with polyester fiberfill. Pack until the body is very, very stiff. Then hand-stitch the opening with heavy-duty thread, using a whip stitch. Repeat this procedure with Mama Bear and Papa Bear.

Bears' faces:

Using the face drawing (Fig. 4) as a guide, draw the bears' features with a pencil, and embroider them with two strands of embroidery floss. Use red for the nose and mouth, working in a back stitch. For the eyes, first stitch the irises to the eyes, and then top-stitch the eyes in place.

Fig. 4

MAKING THE CLOTHES

Papa and Baby:

To make Papa Bear's dickey, cut a small hole in the middle of the 4 x 2½″ (10 x 6.25 cm.) piece and then cut across the middle of the back. Fit it closely around the neck and stitch at the back. Next, cut a strip from the white cotton material ½″ (1.25 cm.) wide and long enough to fit around the neck. Turn under the raw edges, slip it around the neck

and stitch it to the dickey. (Fig. 5). Then hand-stitch the bow tie in place. Do the same for Baby Bear.

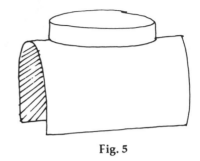

Fig. 5

Next, machine-stitch Papa Bear's vest (B-13, B-14) at the shoulders and side seams. Turn right side out and put on Papa Bear, but don't close it. Repeat this with Baby Bear's vest (B-15, B-16).

Mama Bear:

To make the bib and straps, first take the bib (B-17) and double it, so that you have the same shape as on pattern B-17. Next, fold under ⅛″ (3 mm.) on each side of the straps (B-18), then fold the straps lengthwise, wrong sides facing. Baste the straps to the bib, encasing the raw edges of the sides inside the fold of the straps. (Fig. 6). Machine-stitch

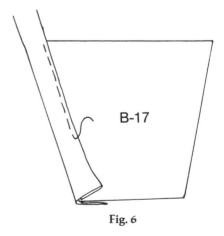

Fig. 6

close to the edge along the entire length of the straps. Remove basting thread. Place on Mama Bear and criss-cross the straps on her back. Stitch the straps to her back, but leave the bib loose for the moment.

BEARS' ASSEMBLY

Lift the vests and the bib up so they don't get stitched with the bodies. Now, using heavy-duty thread and a long needle, begin by pushing the needle through the chest of Baby Bear and out the back, then into Mama Bear from the back and out the chest, across her chest and through again to the back, then into Papa Bear's back, across the chest, and through to the back, then into Baby Bear's back and through to his chest. (Fig. 7). Pull tight and tie with a secure knot. Close the vests and sew a button onto each of them. Then stitch the bib to Mama Bear's waist.

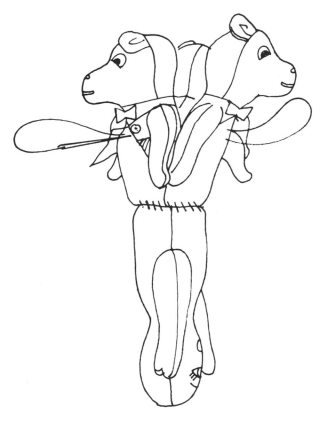

Fig. 7

DOLL ASSEMBLY

Using heavy-duty thread and the whip stitch, hand-stitch Goldilocks to the three bears firmly at the waist so that the doll does not bend. (See Fig. 7).

HAIR

Goldilocks:

Make the bangs by looping the yarn 31 times around a 5 x 3" (12.5 x 7.5 cm.) piece of cardboard. Use the 5" (12.5 cm.) side for looping. Then machine-stitch across one edge at ½" (1.25 cm.) depth. Cut the opposite end (Fig. 8) and remove all the cardboard. Place

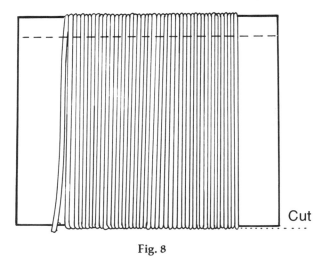

Fig. 8

the yarn at the top of the doll's crown, with the ½" (1.25 cm.) edge over the forehead, forming the bangs. Stitch across the crown and back to secure. Clip the bangs to the correct length. (Fig. 9).

Fig. 9

The braids are made by looping yarn 73 times around a 14 x 6" (35 x 15 cm.) piece of cardboard. Use the 14" (35 cm.) side for looping. Remove the cardboard and machine-stitch down the center, securing the yarn and forming a part. The yarn should now be 7" (17.5 cm.) on either side of the part. Cut across the loops.

Hand-stitch the center of the yarn (the part) to the top of Goldilocks' head, from the forehead to the nape of the neck. Frame the yarn around the face. Hand-stitch the yarn at intervals on the back of the head to secure. Tie a length of thread around the yarn where the braids will start and make the braids, securing them with thread. Clip the ends evenly. (Fig. 10).

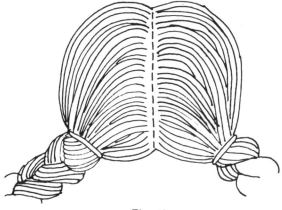

Fig. 10

MAKING THE CLOTHES

Goldilocks' blouse:

Baste and machine-stitch the front (G-2) to the two sections of the back (G-3) at the shoulders, right sides facing. Then, hem the sleeves (G-4) along the straight edge and add the lace. Set the sleeves in the armholes of the blouse, baste and machine-stitch. (Fig. 11). Baste and machine-stitch down the sides of the sleeves.

Match the notches of the front with those of the back sections, baste and machine-stitch down the sides. Fold under the neck and add lace by top-stitching around the neck. Remove all basting thread. Put the blouse on the

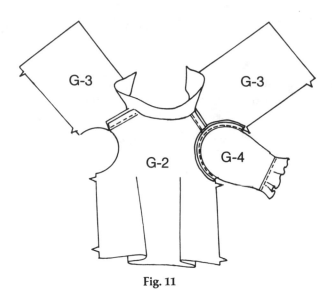

Fig. 11

doll and hemstitch the back closed. Then make folds in the front, as shown in illustration (Fig. 11), and hand-stitch the blouse to the doll at the waist.

Goldilocks' and Bears' skirts:

The skirts for Goldilocks and the three bears are made together. With right sides facing, pin the solid color cotton material to the print cotton material at the hemline, or along the 27" (67.5 cm.) edge. Leave a ¼" (6 mm.) seam and baste it. Remove pins. Machine-stitch the sections together along the hemline. (Fig. 12). Remove basting thread.

Machine-stitch gathering stitches on the other two 27" (67.5 cm.) edges but don't pull to shape as yet. Fold the fabric in half with the right sides facing so that the piece now measures 17½ x 13½" (43.75 x 33.75 cm.) and baste along the 17½" (43.75 cm.) edge. (The previously stitched seam now faces itself.) Measure 2" (5 cm.) in from each end—along basted edge—and mark with pins. (Fig. 13). Next, machine-stitch between these pin marks, back-stitching at the beginning and end to secure the seam. Remove pins and basting thread.

Now turn this tubular piece inside out, wrong side facing, and match the top raw edges as shown in illustration. (Fig. 14). Top-stitch along the hemline. The raw edges become the skirt waistlines. The seams become the center backs of the skirts.

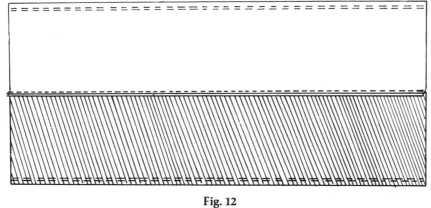

Fig. 12

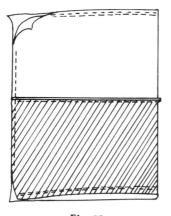

Fig. 13

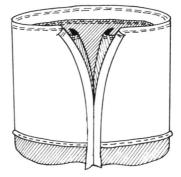

Fig. 14

Goldilocks' and Bears' waistbands:

With right sides facing, fold the print waistband strip—11 x 1¾" (27.5 x 4.5 cm.)—in half lengthwise and machine-stitch each end. Back-stitch to make them secure. Next, turn the piece to the right side and press. Pull to shape the top raw edge of the print skirt to fit the waistband. Turn under one right side raw edge of the band and pin to the right side top raw edge of the print skirt, matching each end with the center-back seam of the skirt. Baste, remove pins and machine-stitch. Remove basting thread.

Flip the waistband over the top of the skirt and, turning under the remaining raw edge of the band, hemstitch it to the other side to encase the top raw edge of the same skirt. (Fig. 15). Repeat this procedure with the solid color waistband to encase the top raw edge of the solid skirt at the waist.

Fig. 15

FINISHING

Put the print skirt on Goldilocks. The seam should be at the back. Hand-stitch the waistband to the doll and hand-stitch the skirt's seam closed. Turn the doll upside down and hand-stitch the other waistband to the three bears. Hand-stitch the skirt's seam closed.

Snow-White and the Seven Dwarfs (see pages 123–135).

Little Boy Blue and the Sheep (see pages 37–52).

Cinderella, Stepmother and Stepsisters (see pages 21–36).

Little Red Riding Hood, Grandmother and the Wolf (see pages 53–65).

Mary and the Little Lamb (see pages 67–82).

Goldilocks and the Three Bears (see pages 83–95).

Little Miss Muffet and the Spider (see pages 111–121).

Mother Hubbard and Her Dog (see pages 97–109).

Peter, Peter and His Wife (see pages 137–154).

Alice, the Mad Hatter and the March Hare (see pages 155–172).

Mother Hubbard and Her Dog

OLD MOTHER HUBBARD
Went to the cupboard,
To fetch her poor dog a bone,
But when she got there,
The cupboard was bare,
And so the poor dog had none.

Mother Hubbard and Her Dog

MATERIALS YOU'LL NEED

¼ yard (22.5 cm.) light pink cotton material—Mother Hubbard's head-and-body (H-1)

½ yard (45 cm.) plush fabric—dog's head-and-body (D-1 through D-4)

A scrap of white felt—dog's eyes (D-5)

A scrap of black felt—dog's eyes (irises) (D-5)

A scrap of red felt—dog's nose (D-6)

A scrap of brown felt—dog's pipe (D-7, D-8)

¼ yard (22.5 cm.) white cotton material—Mother Hubbard's apron and bonnet (H-5, H-6)

½ yard (45 cm.) light color print material—Mother Hubbard's skirt and blouse (H-2, H-3, H-4)

½ yard (45 cm.) tan or brown cotton material—dog's skirt

A scrap of peach-colored felt—dog's bone (D-9)

10-yard (900 cm.) skein of gray rug yarn—Mother Hubbard's hair

1½ yards (135 cm.) medium-width lace—Mother Hubbard's blouse and apron

2 snaps

Black, brown, and red embroidery floss for faces

1½ pounds of polyester fiberfill for stuffing

Note: All seam allowances are ½" (1.25 cm.) for dolls, and ¼" (6 mm.) for clothes.

CUTTING

Mother Hubbard's head-and-body and clothes:

Make the paper patterns from the pattern pieces (H-1 through H-6), enlarging, if needed, to actual size. Cut all pattern pieces from material, remembering to reverse the pattern when pairs are needed.

For Mother Hubbard's skirt, cut a rectangle 36 x 10" (90 x 25 cm.), and a strip 10 x 1¾" (25 x 4.5 cm.) for the waistband.

For Mother Hubbard's apron bottom, cut a rectangle 10 x 6" (25 x 15 cm.), and a strip 17 x 1½" (42.5 x 3.75 cm.) for the band/tie.

For Mother Hubbard's bonnet, cut a strip 20 x 3" (50 x 7.5 cm.) for the ruffle, and another strip 28 x 1½" (70 x 3.75 cm.) for the facing-and-ties (all from white cotton material).

Dog's head-and-body and clothes:

Make the paper patterns from the pattern pieces (D-1 through D-9), enlarging, if needed, to actual size. Cut all pattern pieces from material, remembering to reverse the pattern when pairs are needed.

For the dog's skirt, cut a rectangle 36 x 10" (90 x 25 cm.), and a strip 10 x 1¾" (25 x 4.5 cm.) for the waistband.

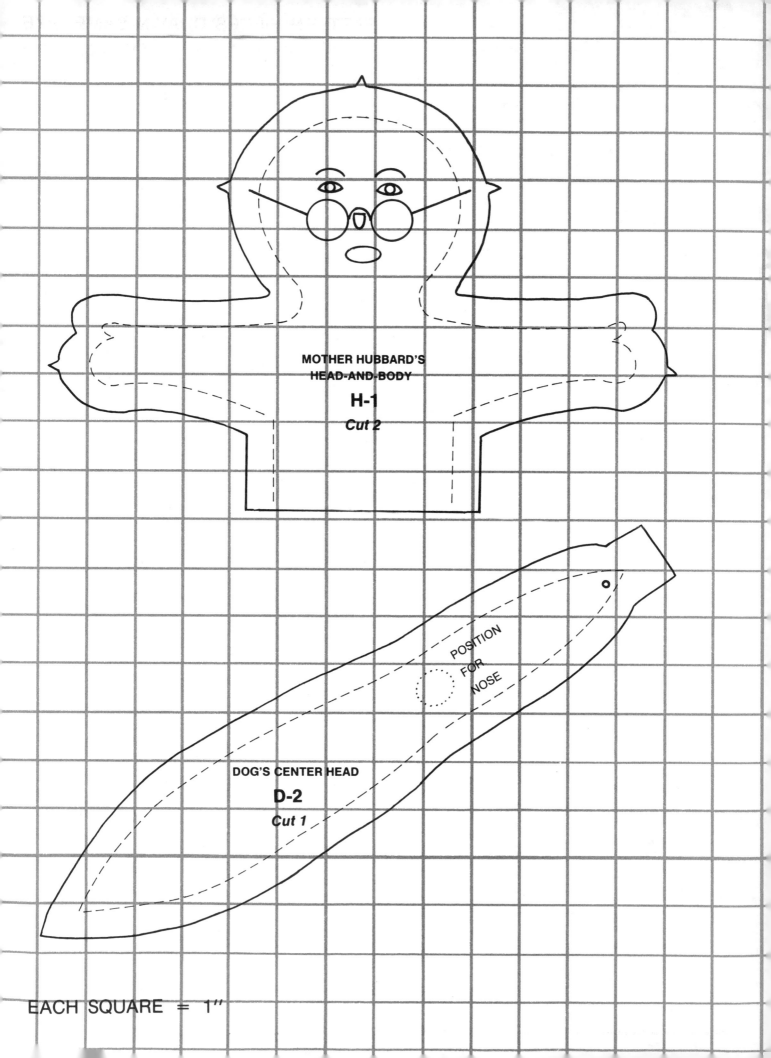

MOTHER HUBBARD'S
HEAD-AND-BODY

H-1

Cut 2

POSITION
FOR
NOSE

DOG'S CENTER HEAD

D-2

Cut 1

EACH SQUARE = 1"

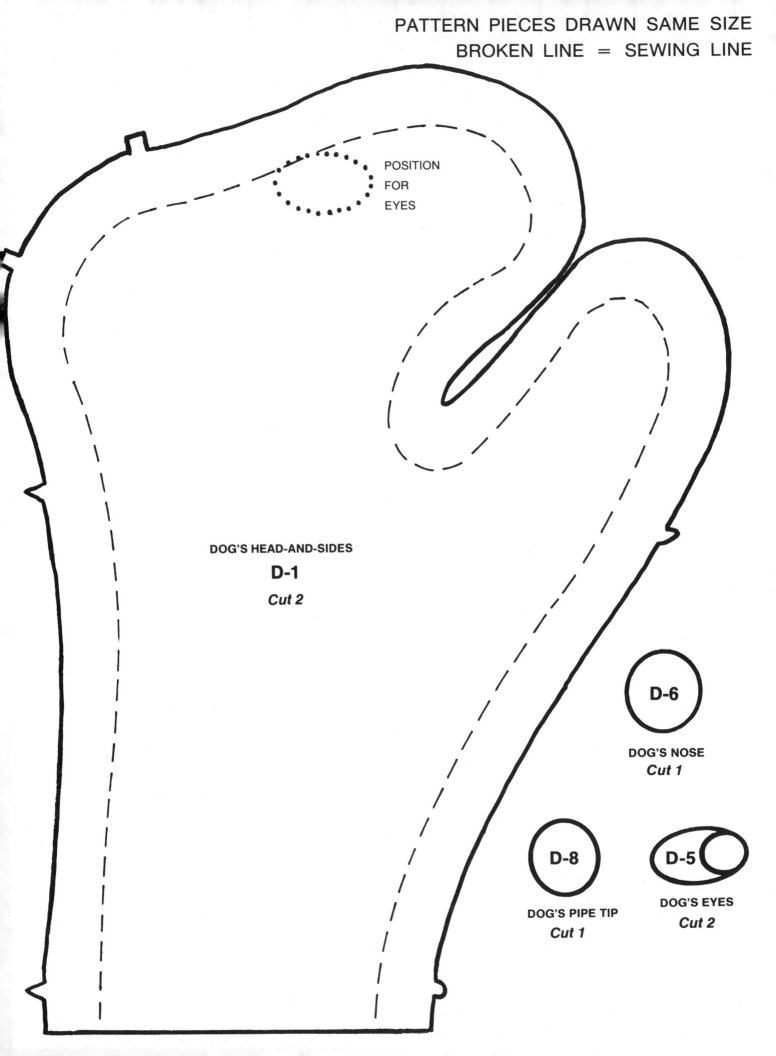

PATTERN PIECES DRAWN SAME SIZE
BROKEN LINE = SEWING LINE

POSITION
FOR
EYES

DOG'S HEAD-AND-SIDES
D-1
Cut 2

D-6

DOG'S NOSE
Cut 1

D-8

DOG'S PIPE TIP
Cut 1

D-5

DOG'S EYES
Cut 2

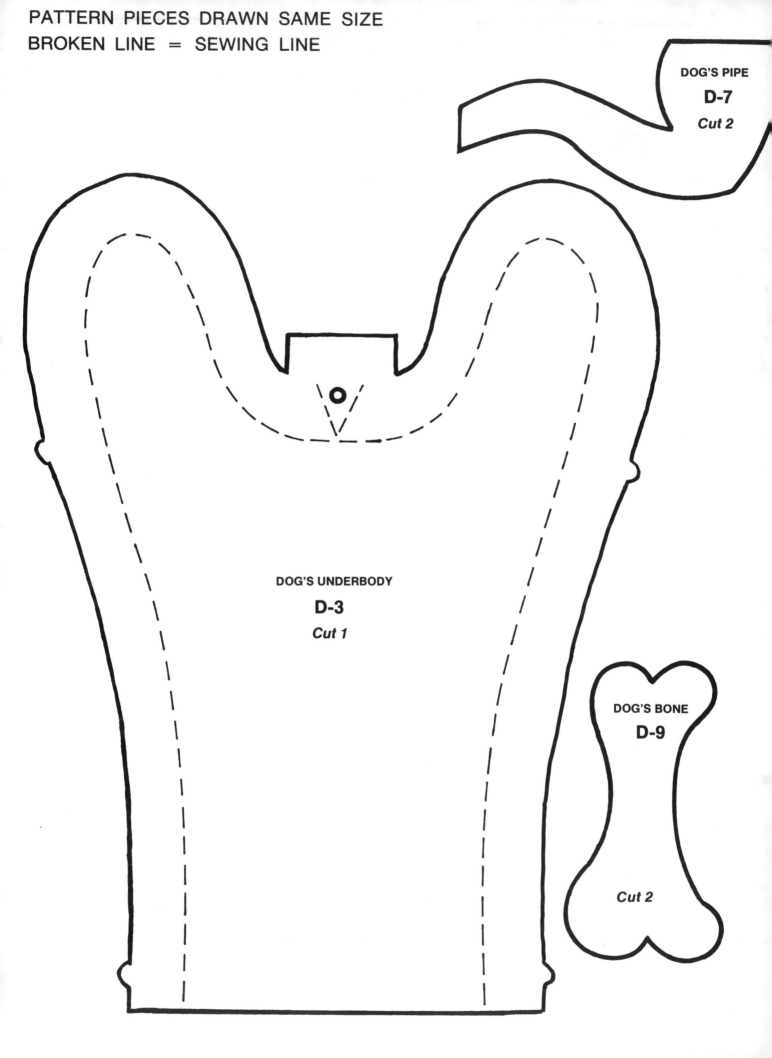

PATTERN PIECES DRAWN SAME SIZE
BROKEN LINE = SEWING LINE

DOG'S PIPE
D-7
Cut 2

DOG'S UNDERBODY
D-3
Cut 1

DOG'S BONE
D-9

Cut 2

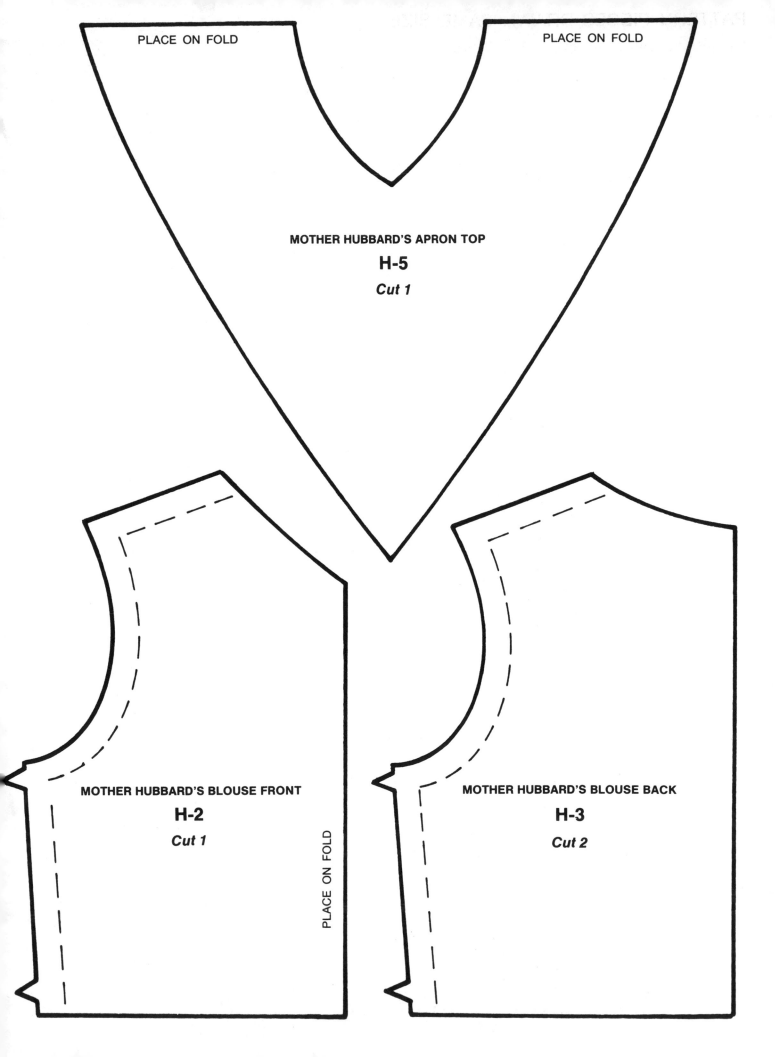

PLACE ON FOLD

PLACE ON FOLD

MOTHER HUBBARD'S APRON TOP

H-5

Cut 1

MOTHER HUBBARD'S BLOUSE FRONT

H-2

Cut 1

PLACE ON FOLD

MOTHER HUBBARD'S BLOUSE BACK

H-3

Cut 2

PLACE ON FOLD

PATTERN PIECES DRAWN SAME SIZE
BROKEN LINE = SEWING LINE

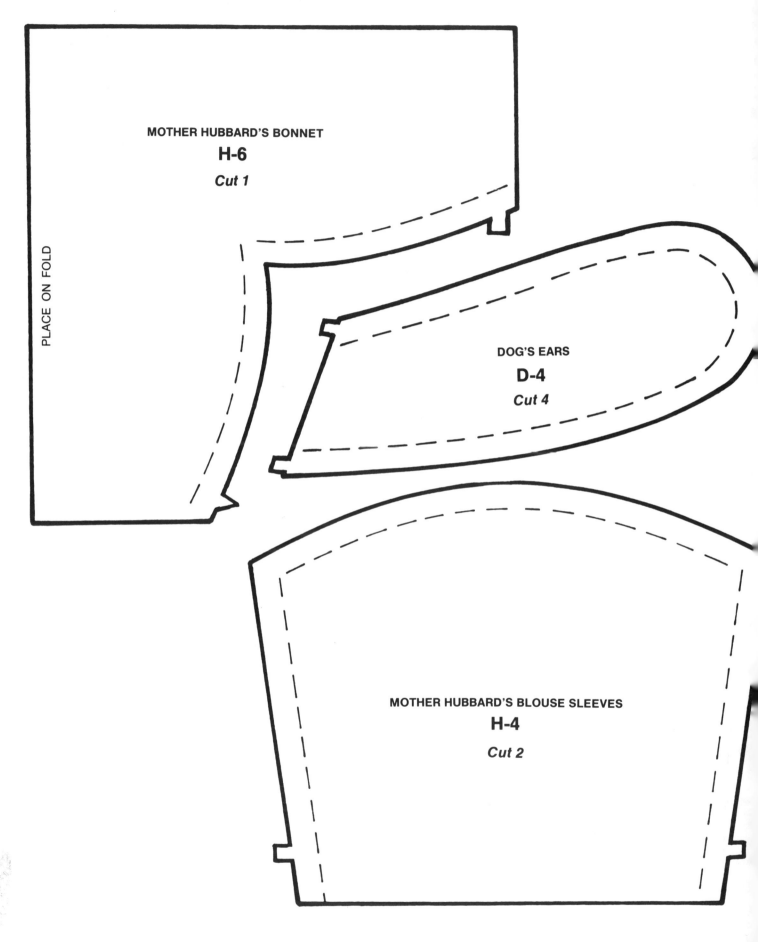

PLACE ON FOLD

MOTHER HUBBARD'S BONNET

H-6

Cut 1

DOG'S EARS

D-4

Cut 4

MOTHER HUBBARD'S BLOUSE SLEEVES

H-4

Cut 2

SEWING AND EMBROIDERING

Mother Hubbard's face:

Using the face drawing (Fig. 1) as a guide, draw Mother Hubbard's face with a pencil onto one of the head-and-body sections.

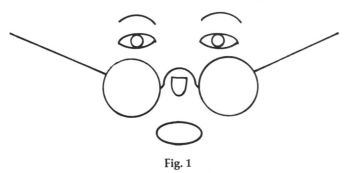

Fig. 1

Then, using an embroidery hoop, embroider the features with two strands of embroidery floss. Use red for the nose and mouth, working in an outline stitch. Use black for the glasses, also working in an outline stitch. The eyebrows and eyes are brown and worked in an outline stitch. The iris is also brown but worked in a satin stitch.

Mother Hubbard's head-and-body:

Match the notches and baste the head-and-body sections (H-1) together, right sides facing. Machine-stitch where indicated on the pattern, leaving the bottom open for stuffing. Remove basting thread. Trim the seams and clip the curves as illustrated. (Fig. 2). Turn the

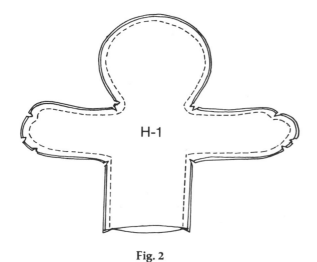

Fig. 2

material right side out and stuff with polyester fiberfill, packing it until the body is very, very stiff. Then hand-stitch the opening with heavy-duty thread, using a whip stitch.

Dog's head-and-body:

With right sides facing, baste and machine-stitch two ear sections (D-4) where marked on the pattern. Remove basting thread and turn right side out. Do the same with the other ear. Then, matching the square notches, place the ears on the right side of the head-and-sides sections (D-1). Baste and machine-stitch.

Now, match the triangular notches of the two head-and-sides sections (D-1), right sides facing. Baste and machine-stitch these two sections as far as the top triangular notch. (Fig. 3). Next, position the underbody (D-3) to one of the D-1 sides, matching the rounded notches. Pin and baste these two sections (D-1 and D-3) together as far as the dot shown in pattern D-3. Remove pins and machine-stitch.

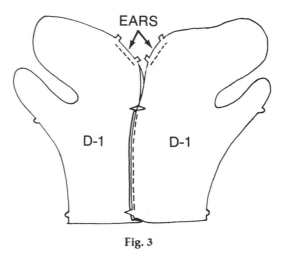

Fig. 3

Then match the dot on the center head section (D-2) with the dot on the underbody (see pattern piece). Now pin the center head section all the way along as shown in illustration. (Fig. 4). Baste, remove pins and machine-stitch. Then, with right sides facing, pin the other head-and-sides section (D-1) to the other side of the underbody (D-2) and center head (D-3) sections. Baste, remove pins and

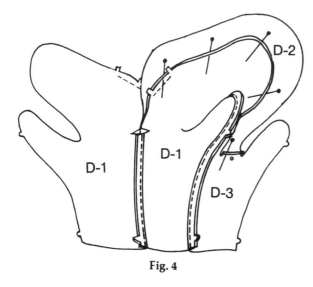

Fig. 4

machine-stitch. Remove all basting thread. Trim the seams and clip the curves.

Turn the material right side out and stuff with polyester fiberfill until the body is very, very stiff. Hand-stitch the opening with heavy-duty thread, using a whip stitch. The ears should be flopping on either side. Stitch them to the head from under the ear, about an inch (2.5 cm.) below the top.

Dog's face:

Top-stitch the black felt irises to the white felt eyes (D-5). (Fig. 5). Then hand-stitch the

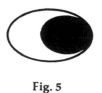

Fig. 5

eyes to the dog. (The position for the eyes is shown by a dotted circle on pattern D-1.) Hand-stitch the red felt nose (D-6) in place. (The position for the nose is shown by a dotted circle on pattern D-2.)

Dog's pipe:

Top-stitch the two pipe sections (D-7), leaving the top open. Then stuff with polyester fiberfill, and top-stitch the pipe top (D-8)

in place. Attach the pipe to the dog's left paw with a snap.

DOLL ASSEMBLY

When attaching the two parts together, turn Mother Hubbard in the same direction as her dog. (Fig 6). Using heavy-duty thread and the whip stitch, hand-stitch Mother Hubbard to the dog firmly at the waist so that the doll does not bend.

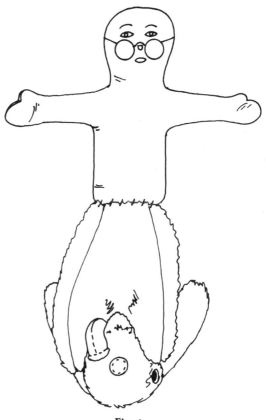

Fig. 6

HAIR

Mother Hubbard

Wind gray rug yarn 40 times around a 6 x 6″ (15 x 15 cm.) piece of cardboard. Machine-stitch across the center to form the part and secure the yarn. (Fig. 7). Remove the cardboard. Place the yarn on top of Mother Hubbard's head, framing the face. Stitch it to

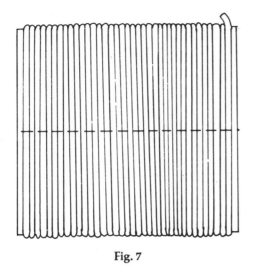

Fig. 7

the top of her head and sides to secure, then stitch all the way across the nape of her neck. (Fig. 8). Cut the loops and trim the ends evenly.

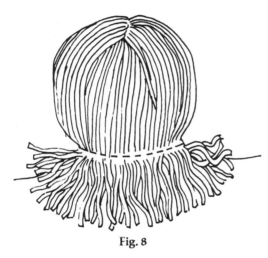

Fig. 8

MAKING THE CLOTHES

Mother Hubbard's bonnet:

With right sides facing, match the left hand square notch with the left hand triangular notch on the bonnet (H-6) and baste where indicated on the pattern. (Fig. 9). Do

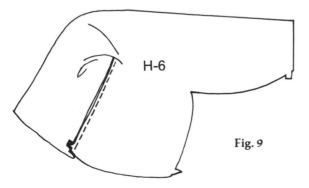

Fig. 9

the same on the other side. Then machine-stitch and remove basting thread. Hem the bottom.

Next, take the ruffle strip, fold it in half lengthwise and gather it to fit the top of the bonnet. Pin the ruffle to the right side of the bonnet. Fold under both sides of the facing-and-ties strip, encase the raw edges of the bonnet top and ruffle and baste. (Fig. 10). Make sure the ties are of equal length on both sides. Remove pins and machine-stitch. The ties should also be machine-stitched. Remove all basting thread and put bonnet on doll.

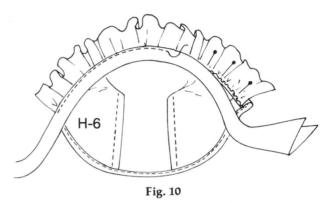

Fig. 10

Mother Hubbard's blouse:

Fold the sleeves (H-4) at the square notches and then fold over, as shown in illustration. (Fig. 11). Gather lace by hand and slip it into the fold. Pin and baste. Remove pins and top-stitch. Next, baste and machine-stitch the back sections (H-3) to the front (H-2) at the shoulders, right sides facing. Turn under the neck and top-stitch lace around it.

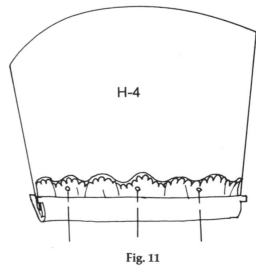

Fig. 11

Set the sleeves (H-4) in the armholes of the blouse, baste and machine-stitch. (Fig. 12). Then baste and machine-stitch down the sides of the sleeves. Finally, match the notches of the back sections to the notches of the front and baste and machine-stitch down the sides. Remove all basting thread. Put the blouse on the doll, hemstitch the back closed, and stitch it at the bottom to secure.

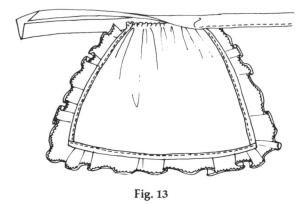

Fig. 13

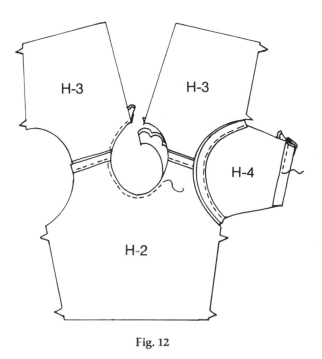

Fig. 12

Mother Hubbard's apron top:

Hem the apron top (H-5) all around the edges and around the neck. Then place it on the doll and secure it with a few stitches at the bottom.

Mother Hubbard's apron bottom:

Hem on three sides—two 6" (15 cm.) sides and one 10" (25 cm.) side—and then gather lace and top-stitch it to these three sides. Gather the remaining 10" (25 cm.) side to fit the doll. Then fold the band/tie in half lengthwise and encase the gathered edge of the apron. Turn under the edges of the band/ tie, baste and machine-stitch. (Fig. 13). Put aside.

Mother Hubbard's and Dog's skirts:

The skirts for Mother Hubbard and her dog are made together. With right sides facing, pin the print cotton material to the solid color cotton material at the hemline, or along the 36" (90 cm.) edge. Leave a ¼" (6 mm.) seam and baste it. Remove pins. Machine-stitch the sections together along the hemline. (Fig. 14). Remove basting thread.

Machine-stitch gathering stitches on the other two 36" (90 cm.) edges but don't pull to shape as yet. Fold the fabric in half with the right sides facing so that the piece now measures 19½ x 18" (48.75 x 45 cm.), and baste along the 19½" (48.75 cm.) edge. (The previously stitched seam now faces itself.) Measure 2" (5 cm.) in from each end—along the basted edge—and mark with pins. (Fig. 15). Next machine-stitch between these pin marks, back-stitching at the beginning and end to secure the seam. Remove pins and basting thread.

Now turn this tubular piece inside out, wrong sides facing, and match the top raw edges as shown in illustration. (Fig. 16). Top-stitch along the hemline. The raw edges become the skirt waistlines. The seams become the center backs of the skirts.

Mother Hubbard's and Dog's waistbands:

With right sides facing, fold the print waistband strip—10 x 1¾" (25 x 4.5 cm.)—in half lengthwise and machine-stitch each end.

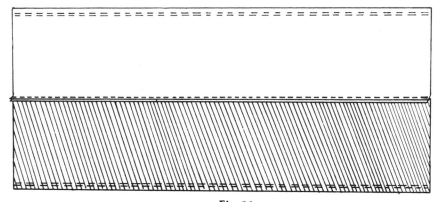

Fig. 14

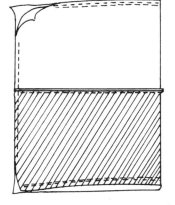

Fig. 15

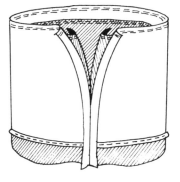

Fig. 16

Back-stitch to make them secure. Next, turn the piece to the right side and press. Pull to shape the top raw edge of the print skirt to fit the waistband. Turn under one right side raw edge of the band and pin to the right side top raw edge of the print skirt, matching each end with the center-back seam of the skirt. Baste, remove pins and machine-stitch. Remove basting thread.

Flip the waistband over the top of the skirt and, turning under the remaining raw edge of the band, hemstitch it to the other side to encase the top raw edge of the same skirt. (Fig. 17). Repeat this procedure with the solid color waistband to encase the top raw edge of the solid color skirt at the waist. Put aside.

Dog's bone:

Top-stitch the two sections of the bone (D-9) all around, leaving an opening for stuffing. Then stuff with polyester fiberfill, and top-stitch the opening. Attach the bone to Mother Hubbard's left hand with a snap.

FINISHING

Put the print skirt on Mother Hubbard. The seam should be at the back. Hand-stitch the waistband to the doll and hand-stitch the skirt's seam closed. Turn the doll upside down and hand-stitch the other waistband to the dog. Hand-stitch the skirt's seam closed. Turn the doll back to Mother Hubbard and tie the apron bottom around the waist.

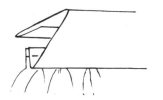

Fig. 17

Little Miss Muffet and the Spider

LITTLE MISS MUFFET
Sat on a tuffet,
Eating her curds and whey;
There came a big spider,
Who sat down beside her
And frightened Miss Muffet away.

Little Miss Muffet and the Spider

MATERIALS YOU'LL NEED

¼ yard (22.5 cm.) light pink cotton material—Miss Muffet's head-and-body (M-1)

¼ yard (22.5 cm.) black felt—spider's head-and-body and legs (S-1)

¼ yard (22.5 cm.) muslin—lining for spider's head-and-body (S-1)

A scrap of light blue felt—spider's eyes

½ yard (45 cm.) cotton print material—Miss Muffet's blouse, skirt and bonnet (M-2 through M-5)

⅓ yard (30 cm.) dark orange cotton material—spider's skirt

A 9 x 12″ (22.5 x 30 cm.) piece of dark orange felt—spider's hat (S-2)

2 yards (180 cm.) white medium-width lace—Miss Muffet's blouse and bonnet

4-ounce skein of dark brown yarn—Miss Muffet's hair

Binding for Miss Muffet's neck ruffle

Black, brown, deep pink, and orange embroidery floss for faces

Sewing thread and heavy-duty thread to match materials

1½ pounds of polyester fiberfill for stuffing

Note: All seam allowances are ½″ (1.25 cm.) for dolls, and ¼″ (6 mm.) for clothes.

CUTTING

Miss Muffet's head-and-body and clothes:

Make the paper patterns from the pattern pieces (M-1 through M-5), enlarging, if needed, to actual size. Cut all pattern pieces from material, remembering to reverse the pattern when pairs are needed.

For Miss Muffet's skirt, cut a rectangle 36 x 12″ (90 x 30 cm.), and a strip 10 x 1¾″ (25 x 4.5 cm.) for the waistband.

For Miss Muffet's blouse, cut a strip 15 x 1½″ (37.5 x 3.75 cm.) for the neck ruffle.

For Miss Muffet's bonnet ruffle, cut a strip 27 x 1¼″ (67.5 x 3 cm.).

Spider's head-and-body and clothes:

Make the paper patterns from the pattern pieces (S-1 and S-2), enlarging, if needed, to actual size. Cut all pattern pieces from material, remembering to reverse the pattern when pairs are needed.

For the spider's skirt, cut a rectangle 36 x 12″ (90 x 30 cm.), and a strip, 10 x 1¾″ (25 x 4.5 cm.) for the waistband.

For the spider's legs, cut eight strips from black felt, each measuring 11 x 2″ (27.5 x 5 cm.).

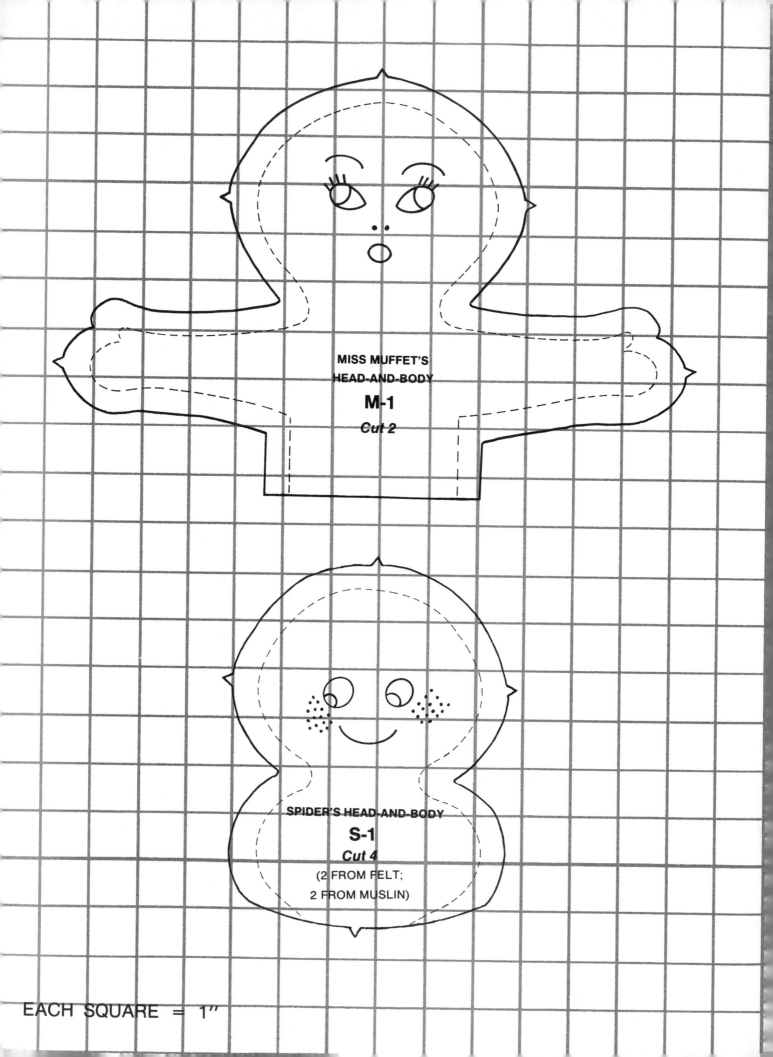

MISS MUFFET'S
HEAD-AND-BODY
M-1
Cut 2

SPIDER'S HEAD-AND-BODY
S-1
Cut 4
(2 FROM FELT;
2 FROM MUSLIN)

EACH SQUARE = 1"

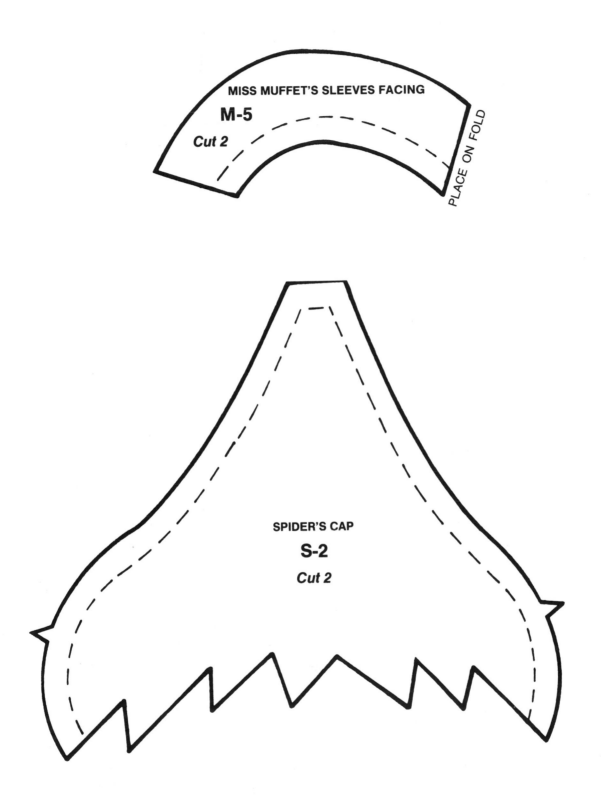

MISS MUFFET'S SLEEVES FACING

M-5

Cut 2

PLACE ON FOLD

SPIDER'S CAP

S-2

Cut 2

PATTERN PIECES DRAWN SAME SIZE

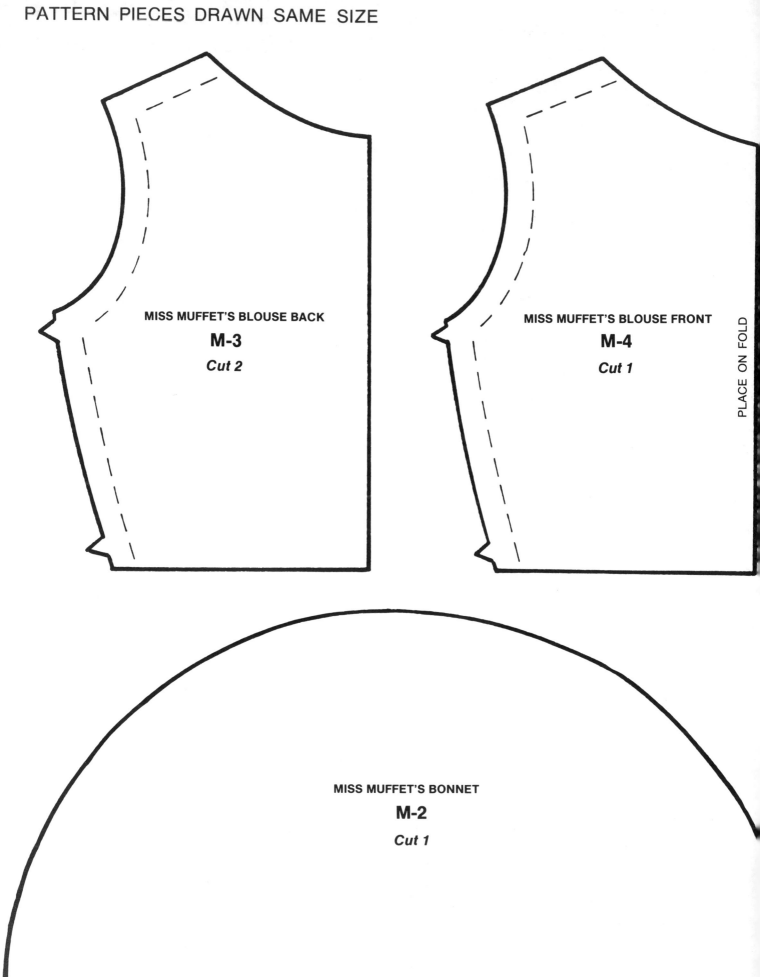

MISS MUFFET'S BLOUSE BACK

M-3

Cut 2

MISS MUFFET'S BLOUSE FRONT

M-4

Cut 1

PLACE ON FOLD

MISS MUFFET'S BONNET

M-2

Cut 1

PLACE ON FOLD

SEWING AND EMBROIDERING

Miss Muffet's face:

Using the face drawing (Fig. 1) as a guide, draw Miss Muffet's face with a pencil onto one of the head-and-body sections. Then,

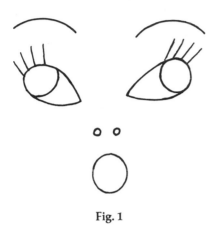

Fig. 1

using an embroidery hoop, embroider the features with a single strand of embroidery floss. Use pink for the nose and mouth, working in an outline stitch. Use brown for the eyes and eyelashes. The eyes are worked in an outline stitch and the eyelashes in a straight stitch. The iris is brown also, but worked in a satin stitch.

Miss Muffet's head-and-body:

Match the notches and baste the head-and-body sections (M-1) together, right sides facing. Machine-stitch where indicated on the pattern, leaving the bottom open for stuffing. Remove basting thread. Trim the seams and clip the curves as illustrated. (Fig. 2). Turn the

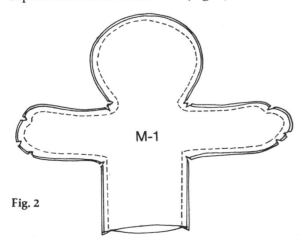

M-1

Fig. 2

material right side out and stuff with polyester fiberfill, packing it until the body is very, very stiff. Then hand-stitch the opening with heavy-duty thread, using a whip stitch.

Spider's face:

Using the face drawing (Fig. 3) as a guide, draw the spider's face with a pencil onto one of the felt head-and-body pieces. Use orange

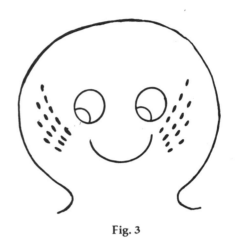

Fig. 3

embroidery floss for the mouth and freckles. Work the mouth in an outline stitch and the freckles in a double stitch. The eyes are made from light blue felt, cut into circles. Black felt is used for the pupils. Sew the eyes to the face.

Spider's head-and-body:

Match the notches and baste the head-and-body sections (S-1) together, the felt right sides facing and the muslin pieces on the outside. Machine-stitch where indicated on the pattern, leaving the bottom open for stuffing. Remove basting thread. Trim the seams and clip the curves. Turn the material right side out and stuff with polyester fiberfill, packing it until the body is very, very stiff. Be careful when you're stuffing, as felt stretches very easily. The muslin lining, however, should give it added protection. Hand-stitch the opening with heavy-duty thread, using a whip stitch.

Spider's legs:

Roll the eight 11 x 2″ (27.5 x 5 cm.) black felt strips together and stitch them. Put aside.

DOLL ASSEMBLY

When attaching the two parts, turn Miss Muffet in the same direction as the spider. (Fig. 4). Using heavy-duty thread and the whip stitch, hand-stitch Miss Muffet to the spider firmly at the waist so that the doll does not bend.

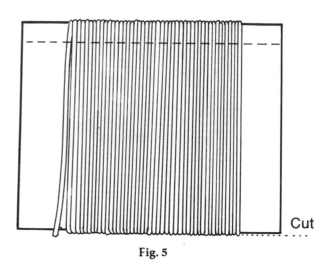

Fig. 5

the yarn at the top of the doll's crown, with the ½″ (1.25 cm.) edge over the forehead, forming the bangs. Stitch across the crown and back to secure. Clip the bangs to the correct length. (Fig. 6).

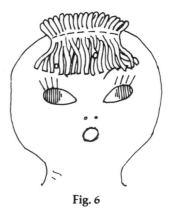

Fig. 6

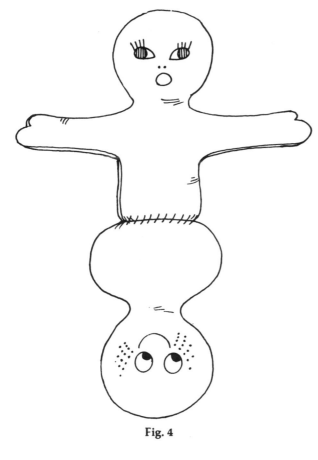

Fig. 4

HAIR

Miss Muffet:

Make the bangs by looping the yarn 31 times around a 5 x 3″ (12.5 x 7.5 cm.) piece of cardboard. Use the 5″ (12.5 cm.) side for looping. Then machine-stitch across one edge at ½″ (1.25 cm.) depth. Cut the opposite end (Fig. 5) and remove all the cardboard. Place

The braids are made by looping yarn 73 times around a 14 x 6″ (35 x 15 cm.) piece of cardboard. Use the 14″ (35 cm.) side for looping. Remove the cardboard and machine-stitch down the center, securing the yarn and forming a part. The yarn should now be 7″ (17.5 cm.) on either side of the part. Cut across the loops.

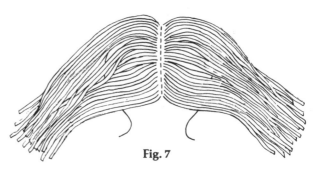

Fig. 7

Hand-stitch the center of the yarn (the part) to the top of Miss Muffet's head (Fig. 7), from the forehead to the nape of the neck. Frame the yarn around the face. Hand-stitch the yarn at intervals on the back of the head to secure. Tie a length of thread around the yarn where the braids will start and make the braids, securing them with thread. (Fig. 8). Clip the ends evenly. Tie orange ribbons to each braid.

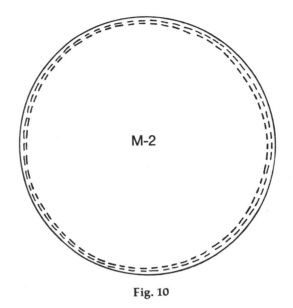

Fig. 10

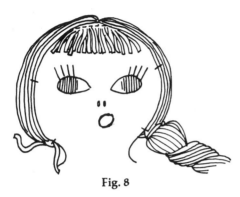

Fig. 8

MAKING THE CLOTHES

Miss Muffet's bonnet:

Hem one edge of the 27 x 1¼" (67.5 x 3 cm.) ruffle strip. Stitch lace to the hemmed edge. On the opposite edge machine-stitch two rows of gathering stitches, and machine-stitch the ends together. (Fig. 9). Pull bonnet ruffle to shape. The ruffle should be large enough to circle around Miss Muffet's head.

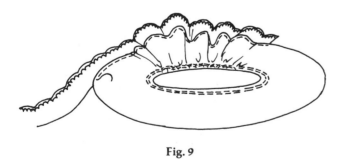

Fig. 9

Then machine-stitch two rows of gathering stitches on the outer edge of the bonnet (M-2). (Fig. 10). Pull to shape. It should be the same size as the ruffle. Turn under the raw edge of the bonnet and hand-stitch it to the

ruffle. (Fig. 11). Stuff the bonnet lightly with polyester fiberfill and stitch it to Miss Muffet's head.

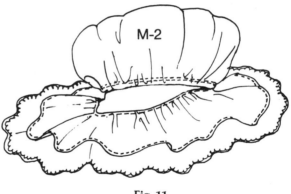

Fig. 11

Miss Muffet's blouse:

Baste and machine-stitch the two sections of the back (M-3) to the front (M-4) at the shoulders, right sides facing. Add the sleeve facing (M-5) at the armholes. Hem one edge of the neck ruffle, the 15 x 1½" (37.5 x 3.75 cm.) strip. Machine-stitch white lace to this hemmed edge. Gather the opposite edge to the size of the neck and machine-stitch it to the neck edge of the blouse. (Fig. 12). Add binding around the neck to conceal the raw edges.

Match the notches of the back to those of the front, then baste and machine-stitch the sides. Remove all basting thread. Fit the

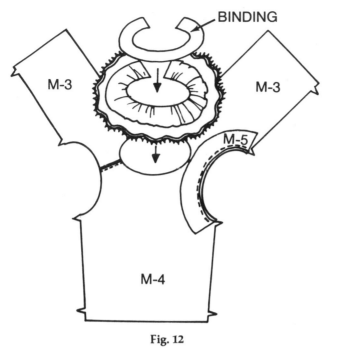

BINDING

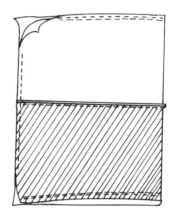

M-3   M-3

M-5

M-4

Fig. 12

Machine-stitch gathering stitches on the other two 36″ (90 cm.) edges but don't pull to shape as yet. Fold the fabric in half with the right sides facing so that the piece now measures 23½ x 18″ (58.75 x 45 cm.) and baste along the 23½″ (58.75 cm.) edge. (The previously stitched seam now faces itself.) Measure 2″ (5 cm.) in from each end—along basted edge—and mark with pins. (Fig. 14).

Fig. 14

blouse on the doll. Turn under the raw edges of the back sections and hemstitch them closed. Slip-stitch the blouse to the doll at the bottom and trim off any excess material. The blouse should have a slightly puffed effect.

Miss Muffet's and Spider's skirts:

The skirts for Miss Muffet and the spider are made together. With right sides facing, pin the solid orange color material to the cotton print material at the hemline, or along the 36″ (90 cm.) edge. Leave a ¼″ (6 mm.) seam and baste it. Remove pins. Machine-stitch the sections together along the hemline. (Fig. 13). Remove basting thread.

Next machine-stitch between these pin marks, back-stitching at the beginning and end to secure the seam. Remove pins and basting thread.

Now turn this tubular piece inside out, wrong sides facing, and match the top raw edges as shown in illustration. (Fig. 15). Top-stitch along the hemline. The raw edges become the skirt waistlines. The seams become the center backs of the skirts.

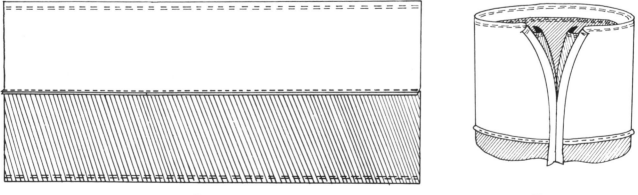

Fig. 13

Fig. 15

Miss Muffet's and Spider's waistbands:

With right sides facing, fold the cotton print waistband strip—10 x 1¾" (25 x 4.5 cm.)—in half lengthwise and machine-stitch each end. Back-stitch to make them secure. Next, turn the piece to the right side and press. Pull to shape the top raw edge of the print skirt to fit the waistband. Turn under one right side raw edge of the band and pin to the right side top raw edge of the print skirt, matching each end with the center-back seam of the skirt. Baste, remove pins and machine-stitch. Remove basting thread.

Flip the waistband over the top of the skirt and, turning under the remaining raw edge of the band, hemstitch it to the other side to encase the top raw edge of the same skirt. (Fig. 16). Repeat this procedure with the orange waistband to encase the top raw edge of the orange skirt at the waist. Put aside.

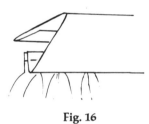

Fig. 16

Spider's hat:

Baste and machine-stitch the two hat sections (S-2) together. Remove basting thread and turn right side out. Fold the peak over (Fig. 17) and stuff lightly with polyester fiberfill. Stitch to the spider's head, using small stitches.

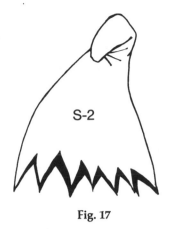

Fig. 17

FINISHING

Put the print skirt on Miss Muffet. The seam should be at the back. Hand-stitch the waistband to the doll and hand-stitch the skirt's seam closed. Turn the doll upside down and hand-stitch the other waistband to the spider. Hand-stitch the skirt's seam closed. Hand-stitch the spider's legs to his body, four on each side as shown in illustration. (Fig. 18). Stitch the legs together here and there to get the curled effect. Finally, hand-stitch Miss Muffet's left arm to her mouth to create the surprised expression.

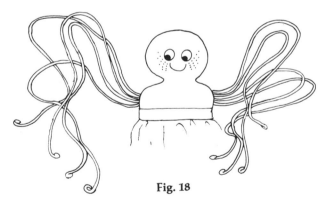

Fig. 18

Snow-White and the Seven Dwarfs

"Mirror, Mirror on the wall,
Who is the fairest of us all?"
"Queen, thou art of beauty rare,
But Snow-White living in the glen
With the seven little men,
Is a thousand times more fair."

Snow-White and the Seven Dwarfs

MATERIALS YOU'LL NEED

¼ yard (22.5 cm.) light pink cotton material—Snow-White's head-and-body (S-1)

¼ yard (22.5 cm.) unbleached muslin material—stepmother's head-and-body (M-1)

¼ yard (22.5 cm.) white and red polka-dot cotton material—Snow-White's yoke, neck band, and sleeves (S-2 through S-4)

½ yard (45 cm.) solid red cotton material—Snow-White's blouse and skirt (S-5, S-6)

½ yard (45 cm.) black cotton material—stepmother's scarf

¾ yard (67.5 cm.) dark print cotton material—stepmother's blouse and skirt (M-2)

A 9 x 12″ (22.5 x 30 cm.) piece of brown felt—stepmother's basket (B-1 through B-3)

A scrap of red felt—apples (B-4)

A 9 x 12″ (22.5 x 30 cm.) piece of white felt—dwarfs' faces (D-1)

A scrap of pink felt—dwarfs' noses

Three 9 x 12″ (22.5 x 30 cm.) pieces of assorted felt—dwarfs' hats and fingers (D-2, D-3)

4-ounce skein of black yarn—Snow-White's hair

10-yard (900 cm.) skein of gray rug yarn—stepmother's hair

2-ounce skein of white baby yarn—dwarfs' beards

1 yard (90 cm.) ribbon to match blouse and skirt—Snow-White's hair

1 yard (90 cm.) narrow white lace—Snow-White's blouse

7 snaps

Black, red, and blue embroidery floss for faces

Sewing thread and heavy-duty thread to match materials

1½ pounds of polyester fiberfill for stuffing

Note: All seam allowances are ½″ (1.25 cm.) for dolls, and ¼″ (6 mm.) for clothes, unless otherwise indicated.

CUTTING

Snow-White's head-and-body and clothes:

Make the paper patterns from the pattern pieces (S-1 through S-6), enlarging, if needed, to actual size. Cut all pattern pieces from material, remembering to reverse the pattern when pairs are needed.

For Snow-White's skirt, cut a rectangle 36 x 12″ (90 x 30 cm.), and a strip 10 x 1¾″ (25 x 4.5 cm.) for the waistband.

For Snow-White's blouse, cut a band 7½ x 1″ (18.75 x 2.5 cm.) on the bias from the red polka-dot material.

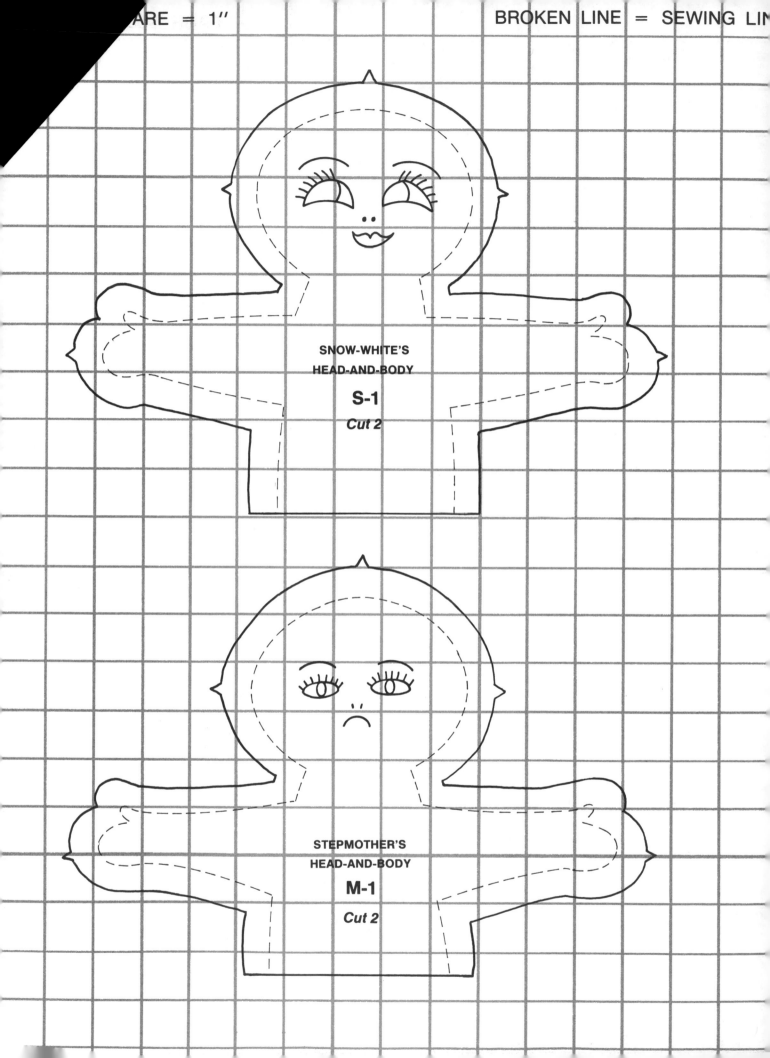

ARE = 1" BROKEN LINE = SEWING LIN

SNOW-WHITE'S
HEAD-AND-BODY

S-1

Cut 2

STEPMOTHER'S
HEAD-AND-BODY

M-1

Cut 2

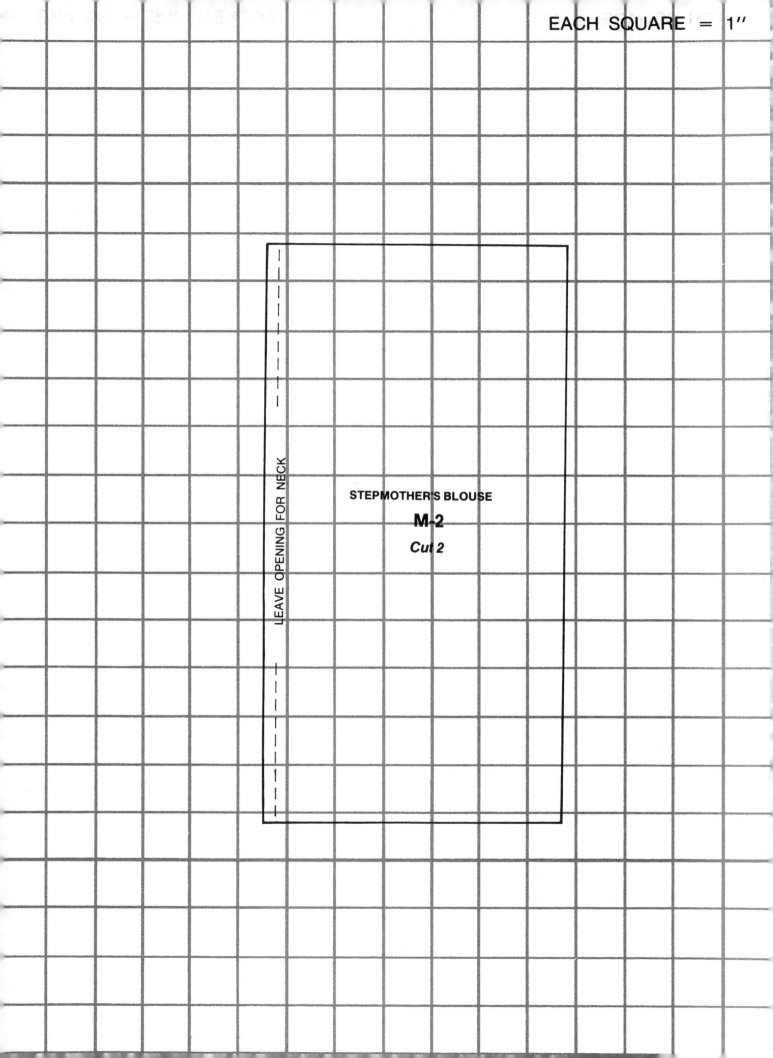

EACH SQUARE = 1"

LEAVE OPENING FOR NECK

STEPMOTHER'S BLOUSE

M-2

Cut 2

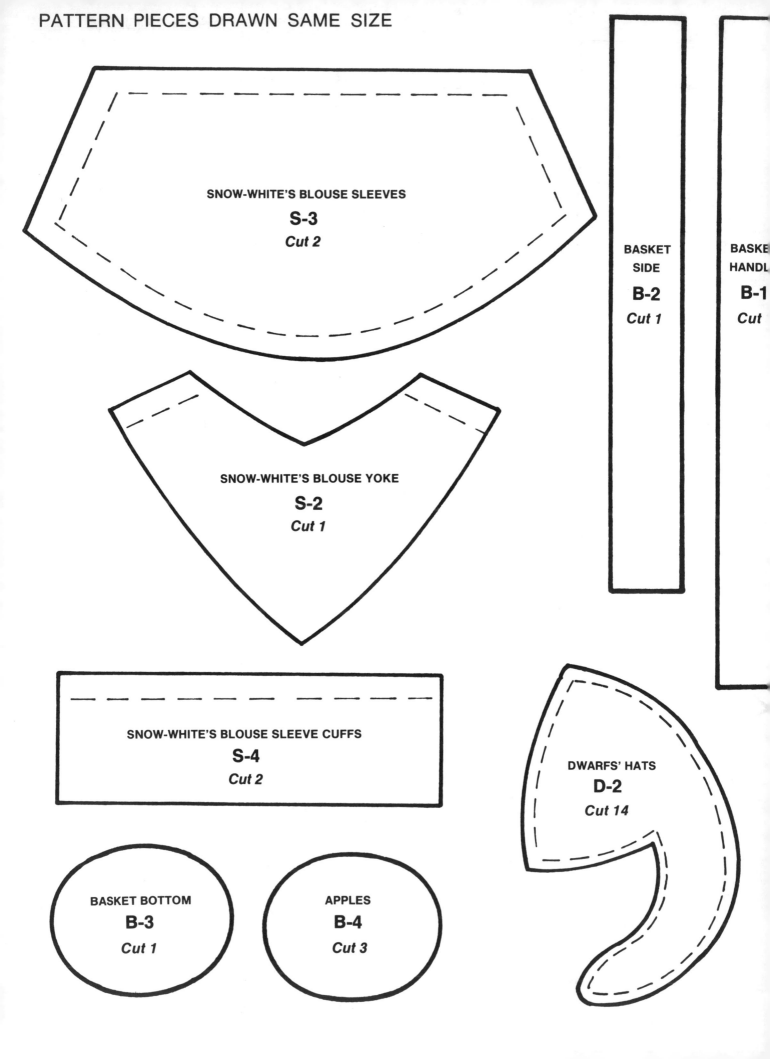

PATTERN PIECES DRAWN SAME SIZE

SNOW-WHITE'S BLOUSE SLEEVES

S-3

Cut 2

BASKET
SIDE

B-2

Cut 1

BASKE
HANDL

B-1

Cut

SNOW-WHITE'S BLOUSE YOKE

S-2

Cut 1

SNOW-WHITE'S BLOUSE SLEEVE CUFFS

S-4

Cut 2

DWARFS' HATS

D-2

Cut 14

BASKET BOTTOM

B-3

Cut 1

APPLES

B-4

Cut 3

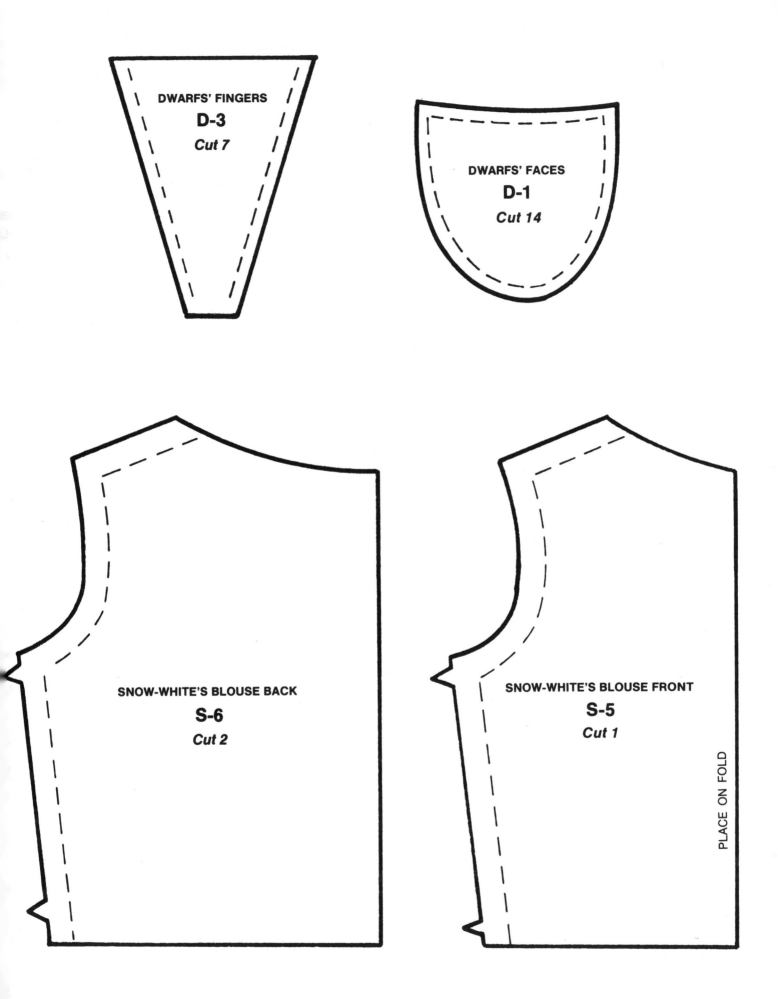

BROKEN LINE = SEWING LINE

DWARFS' FINGERS
D-3
Cut 7

DWARFS' FACES
D-1
Cut 14

SNOW-WHITE'S BLOUSE BACK
S-6
Cut 2

SNOW-WHITE'S BLOUSE FRONT
S-5
Cut 1

PLACE ON FOLD

Stepmother's head-and-body and clothes:

Make the paper patterns from the pattern pieces (M-1, M-2), enlarging, if needed, to actual size. Cut all pattern pieces from material, remembering to reverse the pattern when pairs are needed.

For the stepmother's skirt, cut a rectangle 36 x 12″ (90 x 30 cm.), and a strip 10 x 1¾″ (25 x 4.5 cm.) for the waistband.

For the stepmother's scarf, cut half a 14″ (35 cm.) square on the bias. This will give you a triangle with two 14″ (35 cm.) sides.

Dwarfs' faces, hats and fingers:

Make the paper patterns from the pattern pieces (D-1, D-2, D-3). Cut all pattern pieces from material.

SEWING AND EMBROIDERING

Snow-White's face:

Using the face drawing (Fig. 1) as a guide, draw Snow-White's face with a pencil onto one of the head-and-body sections. Then,

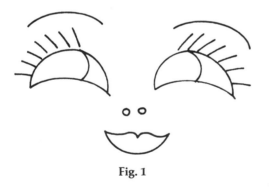

Fig. 1

using an embroidery hoop, embroider the features with a single strand of embroidery floss. Use red for the nose and mouth. The nose is worked in an outline stitch and the mouth in a satin stitch. Use black for the eyes, eyebrows and eyelashes with the eyes and eyebrows worked in an outline stitch and the eyelashes worked in a straight stitch. The iris is blue and worked in a satin stitch.

Snow-White's head-and-body:

Match the notches and baste the head-and-body sections (S-1) together, right sides facing. Machine-stitch where indicated on the pattern, leaving the bottom open for stuffing. Remove basting thread. Trim the seams and clip the curves as illustrated. (Fig. 2). Turn the material right side out and stuff with polyester fiberfill, packing it until the body is very, very stiff. Then hand-stitch the opening with heavy-duty thread, using a whip stitch.

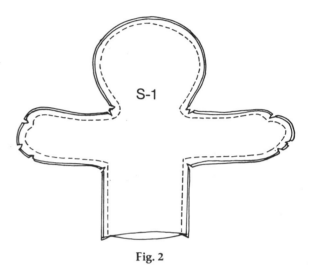

Fig. 2

Stepmother's face:

Using the face drawing (Fig. 3) as a guide, draw the stepmother's face with a pencil onto one of the head-and-body sections. Then,

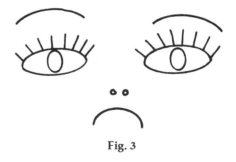

Fig. 3

using an embroidery hoop, embroider the features with a single strand of embroidery floss. Use red for the nose and mouth, working in an outline stitch. Use black for the eyes, eyebrows and eyelashes. The eyes and eyebrows are worked in an outline stitch, the eyelashes in a straight stitch. The iris is black also, but worked in a satin stitch.

Stepmother's head-and-body:

Match the notches and baste the head-and-body sections (M-1) together, right sides facing. Machine-stitch where indicated on the pattern, leaving the bottom open for stuffing. Remove basting thread. Trim the seams and clip the curves. Turn the material right side out and stuff with polyester fiberfill, packing it until the body is very, very stiff. Then hand-stitch the opening with heavy-duty thread, using a whip stitch.

DOLL ASSEMBLY

When attaching the two parts, turn Snow-White in the same direction as the stepmother. (Fig. 4). Using heavy-duty thread and the whip stitch, hand-stitch Snow-White to the stepmother firmly at the waist so that the doll does not bend.

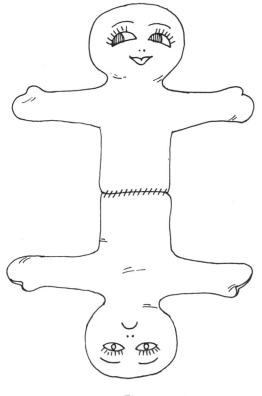

Fig. 4

HAIR

Snow-White:

Make the bangs by looping the black yarn 40 times around a 4 x 4" (10 x 10 cm.) piece of cardboard. Then machine-stitch across both edges at ½" (1.25 cm.) depth and machine-stitch at 1½" (3.75 cm.) depth on one side only. (Fig. 5). Remove the cardboard and cut

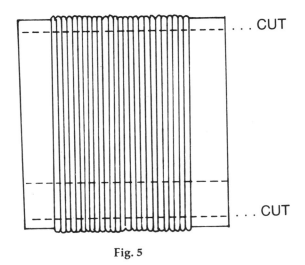

Fig. 5

across loops. Place the double-stitched side at the back of the head and bring the yarn over the face so that the 1½" (3.75 cm.) depth stitching rests across the middle of the forehead. Stitch the yarn at the back of the head and across the forehead at the stitching. (Fig. 6). Then fold the yarn back and stitch to the back of the head. (Fig. 7).

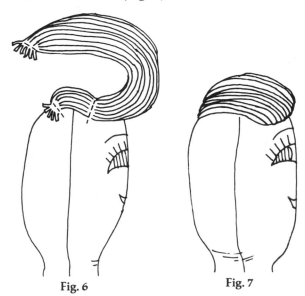

Fig. 6   **Fig. 7**

The second part of the hair is made by wrapping yarn 73 times around a 14 x 6″ (35 x 15 cm.) piece of cardboard. Wrap the yarn around the 14″ (35 cm.) side. Remove the cardboard and machine-stitch across the center, securing the yarn and forming a part. The yarn should now be 7″ (17.5 cm.) on either side of the part.

Place the yarn over Snow-White's head. You should have about ¾″ (2 cm.) of the bangs showing. Then stitch to Snow-White's head, from the forehead to the nape of the neck. Stitch the yarn along the nape of the neck and at intervals on the back of the head and sides to secure. Cut the loops. (Fig. 8). Tie a ribbon at the crown of the head.

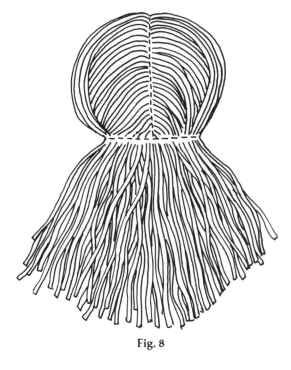

Fig. 8

Stepmother:

The stepmother's hair is done like the second part of Snow-White's hair. The stepmother has no bangs. Also, the hair should be brought forward a bit to frame the face.

MAKING THE CLOTHES

Snow-White's blouse:

First turn under the raw edges of the yoke (S-2). Baste and machine-stitch the yoke to the front (S-5) of the blouse. Remove basting thread. Top-stitch lace to the edge of the yoke. Then baste and machine-stitch the front (S-5) to the two sections of the back (S-6) at the shoulders, right sides facing. (The yoke would also be stitched in with the shoulders.)

Turn under one raw edge of a cuff (S-4) and baste to the inside of the sleeve. Gather the sleeve a little as you baste to fit the cuff. Then machine-stitch. Fold the cuff over the sleeve's edge and turn under the raw edge. Add gathered lace at the top edge and complete the cuff by machine-stitching. Repeat with the second sleeve cuff.

Gather the rounded edge of the sleeves and baste and machine-stitch to the blouse at the armholes. Then fold the neck band in half lengthwise and turn under the raw edges. Encase the raw edges of the neck, and baste and machine-stitch to form the collar. (Fig. 9).

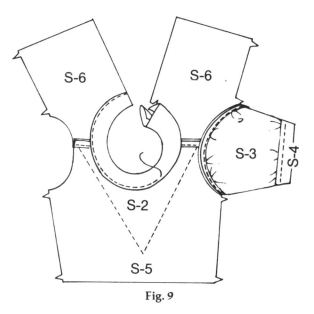

Fig. 9

To complete the blouse, baste and machine-stitch down the sleeves and baste and machine-stitch the back sections to the front, matching notches. Remove all basting thread. Finally fit the blouse to the doll, with pleats at the front and back, and hemstitch up the back.

Snow-White's and Stepmother's skirts:

The skirts for Snow-White and the stepmother are made together. With right sides facing, pin the solid color cotton material to the print cotton material at the hemline, or along the 36″ (90 cm.) edge. Leave a ¼″ (6 mm.) seam and baste it. Remove pins. Machine-stitch the sections together along the hemline. (Fig. 10). Remove basting thread.

Machine-stitch gathering stitches on the other two 36″ (90 cm.) edges but don't pull to shape as yet. Fold the fabric in half with the right sides facing so that the piece now measures 23½ x 18″ (58.75 x 45 cm.) and baste along the 23½″ (58.75 cm.) edge. (The previously stitched seam now faces itself.) Measure 2″ (5 cm.) in from each end—along basted edge—and mark with pins. (Fig. 11). Next machine-stitch between these pin marks, back-stitching at the beginning and end to secure the seam. Remove pins and basting thread.

Now turn this tubular piece inside out, wrong sides facing, and match the top raw edges as shown in illustration. (Fig. 12). Top-stitch along the hemline. The raw edges become the skirt waistlines. The seams become the center backs of the skirts.

Snow-White's and Stepmother's waistbands:

With right sides facing, fold the solid color waistband strip—10 x 1¾″ (25 x 4.5 cm.)—in half lengthwise and machine-stitch each end. Back-stitch to make them secure. Next, turn the piece to the right side and press. Pull to shape the top raw edge of the solid color skirt to fit the waistband. Turn under one right side raw edge of the band and pin to the right side top raw edge of the solid color skirt, matching each end with the center-back seam of the skirt. Baste, remove pins and machine-stitch. Remove basting thread.

Flip the waistband over the top of the skirt and, turning under the remaining raw edge of the band, hemstitch it to the other side to encase the top raw edge of the same skirt. (Fig. 13). Repeat this procedure with the print cotton waistband to encase the top raw edge of the print skirt. Put aside.

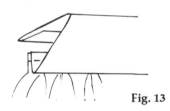

Fig. 13

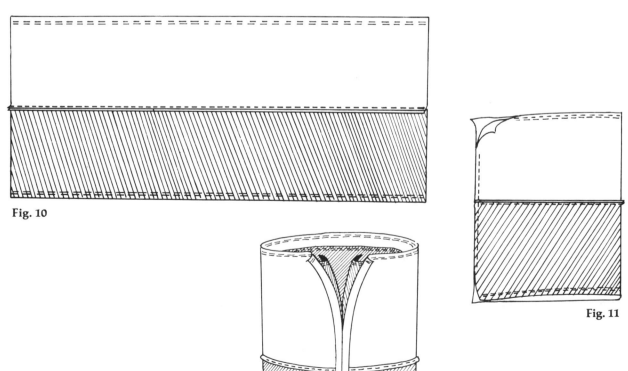

Fig. 10

Fig. 11

Fig. 12

Stepmother's scarf:

Hem the edges of the black cotton material. Place the bias cut edge on the stepmother's head like a babushka. Hand-stitch to the top of the head and on both sides of the face to secure.

Stepmother's blouse:

Baste and machine-stitch the two sections (M-2) across the shoulders as marked on pattern. Leave the neck section open. Remove basting thread. Then hem the neck and sides and slip the blouse over the doll. Stitch the back and front tightly at the wrist. Fold the excess material and stitch at the neck. (Fig. 14).

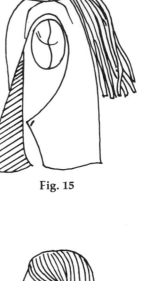

Fig. 15

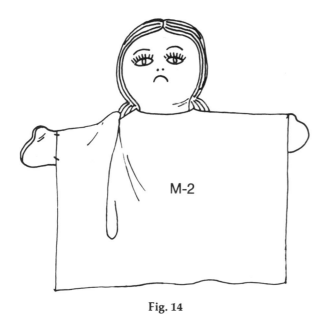

Fig. 14

Fig. 16

Then take the back flap at the bottom on one side and stitch it to the front of the doll. (Fig. 15). Take the front flap at the bottom and stitch it to the back of the doll. (Fig. 16). Repeat with the other side. Finally hand-stitch the blouse to the doll at the base.

Stepmother's basket:

Hemstitch the basket side (B-2) to the bottom (B-3). Stitch the handle (B-1) to the basket. Then gather each apple section (B-4),

stuff lightly with polyester fiberfill and stitch them closed. Hand-stitch apples to the bottom of the basket. Put aside.

Dwarfs' beards:

Wind white baby yarn 35 times around a 3 x 1½" (7.5 x 3.75 cm.) piece of cardboard. Use the 1½" (3.75 cm.) edge for looping. Machine-stitch across one edge at ¼" (6 mm.) depth and cut loops at the other end. Remove the cardboard. Make another six of these.

Dwarfs' faces:

Take the two sections of the face (D-1) and insert a beard all around the curved edge. Then baste and machine-stitch on top with a zigzag stitch, but leave the straightish edge open. Remove basting thread. Stuff lightly with polyester fiberfill and machine-stitch across the open edge.

Next, using the face drawing (Fig. 17) as a guide, draw the eyes and eyebrows with a black magic marker and the mouth with a red

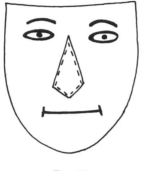

Fig. 17

magic marker. Then cut a piece of pink felt in the shape given in the illustration and stitch it to the face, using small, even stitches. Do the same with the other six dwarfs. (You can draw the eyes and mouths differently to get different expressions.)

Dwarfs' hats:

Take the two sections of the hat (D-2), baste and machine-stitch in a zigzag stitch all around the very curved edges. Remove basting thread. Stuff lightly with polyester fiberfill. Then insert ¼" (6 mm.) of the straightish edge of the dwarf's face between the hat pieces. Machine-stitch across and make sure it is secure. Hand-stitch snaps to the back of the hat. (Fig. 18). Repeat with the other dwarfs.

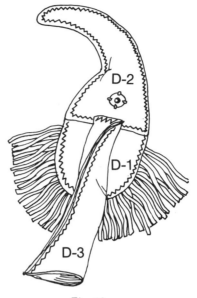

Fig. 18

Dwarfs' fingers:

Take a finger section (D-3), fold it in half lengthwise and machine-stitch on top with a zigzag stitch. Then twist it slightly on top as shown in illustration (Fig. 18) and stitch it to the base of the hat at the back. Repeat with the other dwarf's fingers.

FINISHING

Put the red skirt on Snow-White. The seam should be at the back. Hand-stitch the waistband to the doll and hand-stitch the skirt's seam closed. Hand-stitch the other half of the snaps at intervals around the skirt. The snaps should be about 6" (15 cm.) from the bottom of the skirt. Attach the dwarfs. Turn the doll upside down and hand-stitch the other waistband to the body of the step-mother. Hand-stitch the skirt's seam closed. Finally, loop the basket handle on the step-mother's left arm, and hand-stitch that arm to her body.

Peter, Peter and His Wife

PETER, PETER pumpkin eater,
Had a wife and couldn't keep her;
He put her in a pumpkin shell
And there he kept her very well.

Peter, Peter and His Wife

MATERIALS YOU'LL NEED

½ yard (45 cm.) unbleached muslin—Peter's and wife's head-and-body (P-1 through P-4 and W-1 through W-4)

1 yard (90 cm.) dark cotton print material—wife's blouse, skirt and bonnet (W-5 through W-7)

½-¾ yard (45-67.5 cm.) orange felt—Peter's pumpkin skirt (P-5)

¾ yard (67.5 cm.) solid color cotton material to match print material—Peter's shirt, vest lining, waistband, wife's apron, bonnet lining (P-6 through P-11 and W-5, W-6)

¼ yard (22.5 cm.) dark brown corduroy—Peter's vest (P-10, P-11)

4-ounce skein of brown yarn—Peter's and wife's hair

6 small white buttons

Black, red, light blue, and dark blue embroidery floss for faces

Sewing thread and heavy-duty thread to match materials

1½ pounds of polyester fiberfill for stuffing

Note: All seam allowances are ½" (1.25 cm.) for dolls, and ¼" (6 mm.) for clothes.

CUTTING

Peter's head-and-body and clothes:

Make the paper patterns from the pattern pieces (P-1 through P-11), enlarging, if needed, to actual size. Cut all pattern pieces from material, remembering to reverse the pattern when pairs are needed.

For Peter's skirt waistband, cut a strip 11 x 1¾" (27.5 x 4.5 cm.) from the solid color cotton material.

Wife's head-and-body and clothes:

Make the paper patterns from the pattern pieces (W-1 through W-7), enlarging, if needed, to actual size. Cut all pattern pieces from material, remembering to reverse the pattern when pairs are needed.

For the wife's skirt, cut a rectangle 36 x 12" (90 x 30 cm.), and a strip 11 x 1¾" (27.5 x 4.5 cm.) for the waistband.

For the wife's apron, cut a rectangle 16 x 9" (40 x 22.5 cm.), a strip 5 x 1" (12.5 x 2.5 cm.), and two strips 11 x ½" (27.5 x 1.25 cm.) from the solid color cotton material.

For the wife's bonnet, cut two strips 12 x 1" (30 x 2.5 cm.) from the print material.

PATTERN PIECES DRAWN SAME SIZE

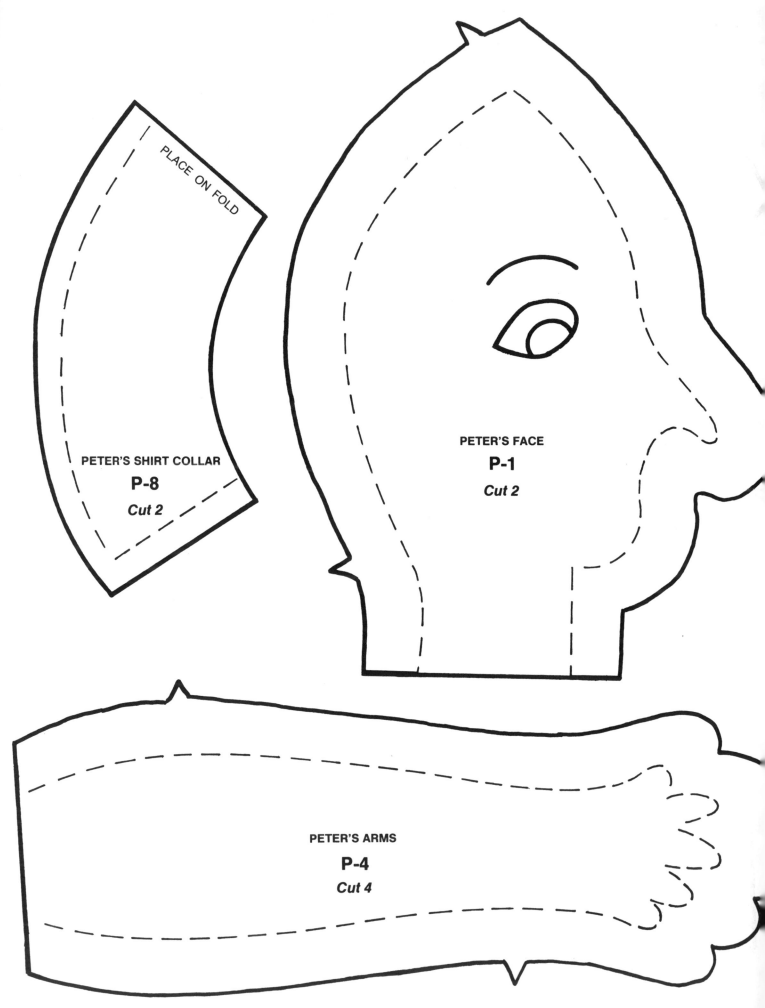

PLACE ON FOLD

PETER'S SHIRT COLLAR
P-8
Cut 2

PETER'S FACE
P-1
Cut 2

PETER'S ARMS
P-4
Cut 4

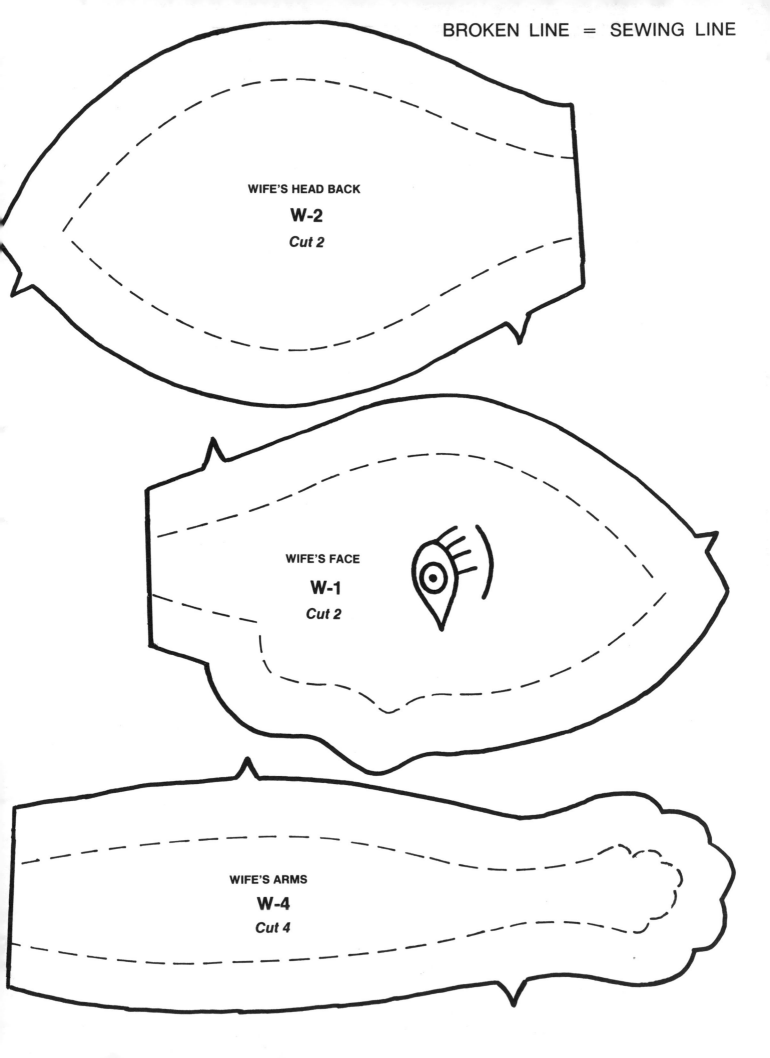

BROKEN LINE = SEWING LINE

WIFE'S HEAD BACK

W-2

Cut 2

WIFE'S FACE

W-1

Cut 2

WIFE'S ARMS

W-4

Cut 4

PATTERN PIECES DRAWN SAME SIZE

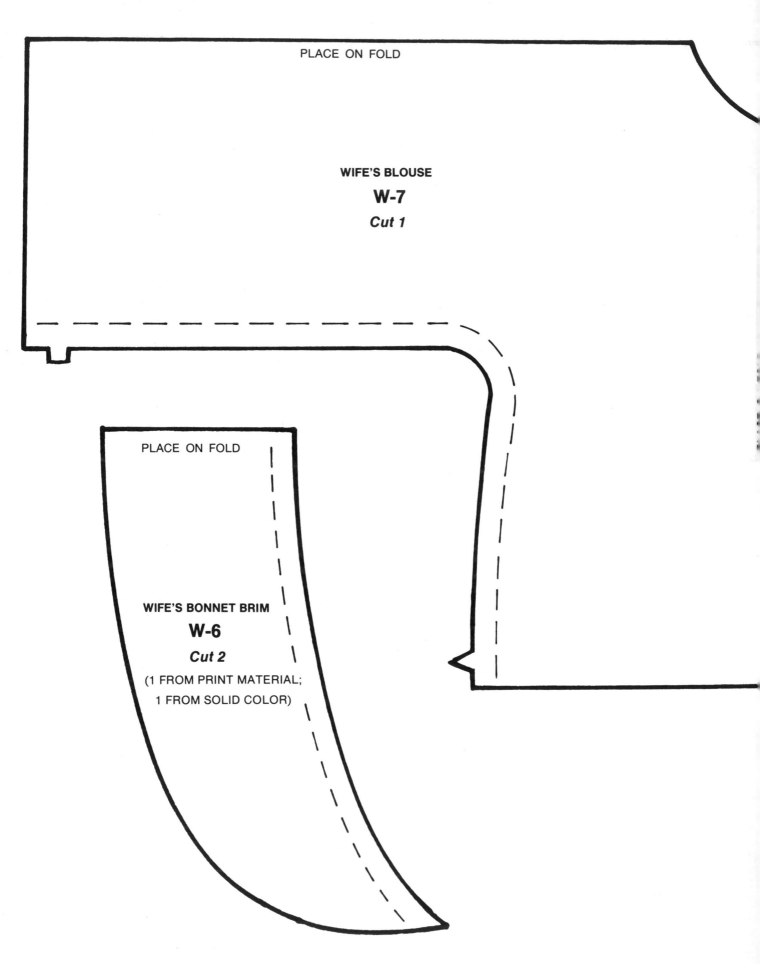

PLACE ON FOLD

WIFE'S BLOUSE

W-7

Cut 1

PLACE ON FOLD

WIFE'S BONNET BRIM

W-6

Cut 2

(1 FROM PRINT MATERIAL;
1 FROM SOLID COLOR)

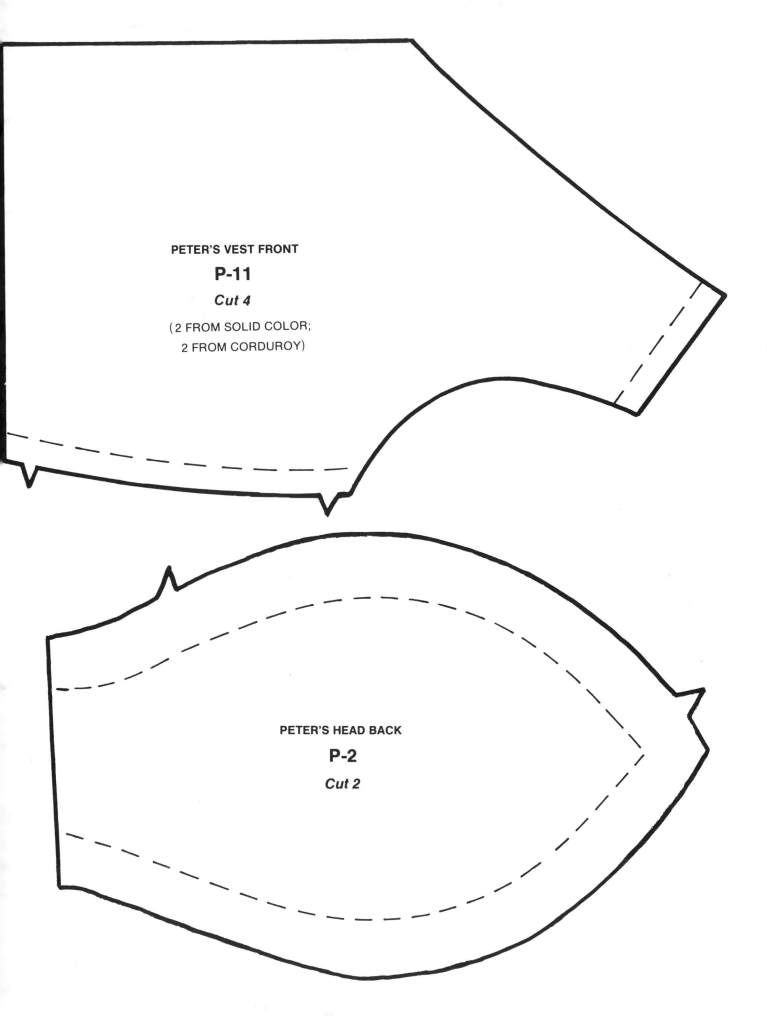

PETER'S VEST FRONT

P-11

Cut 4

(2 FROM SOLID COLOR;
2 FROM CORDUROY)

PETER'S HEAD BACK

P-2

Cut 2

PATTERN PIECES DRAWN SAME SIZE

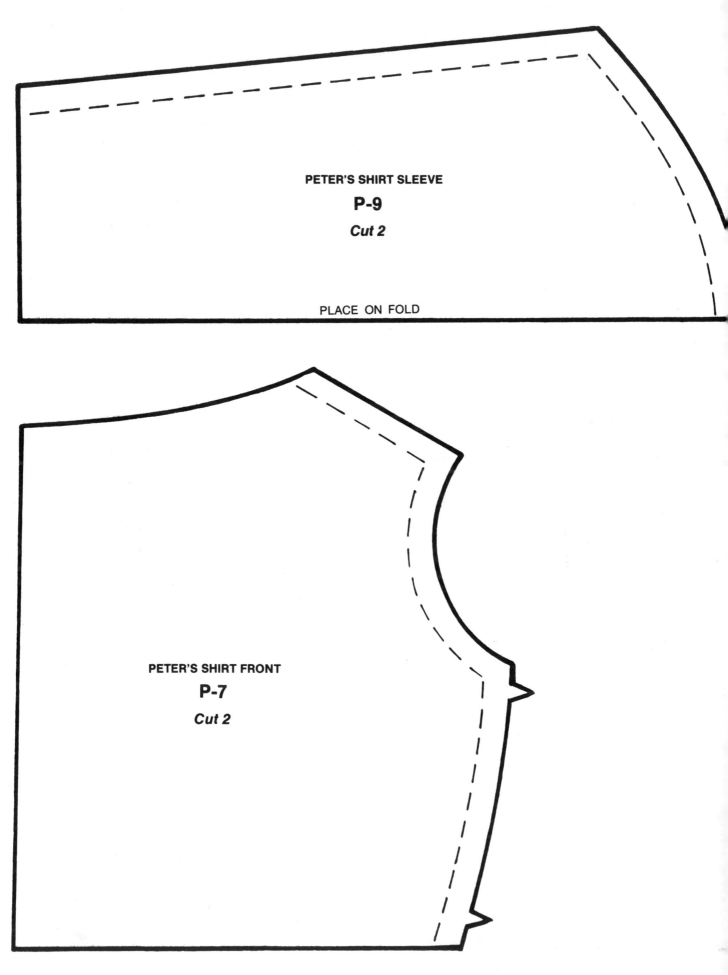

PETER'S SHIRT SLEEVE

P-9

Cut 2

PLACE ON FOLD

PETER'S SHIRT FRONT

P-7

Cut 2

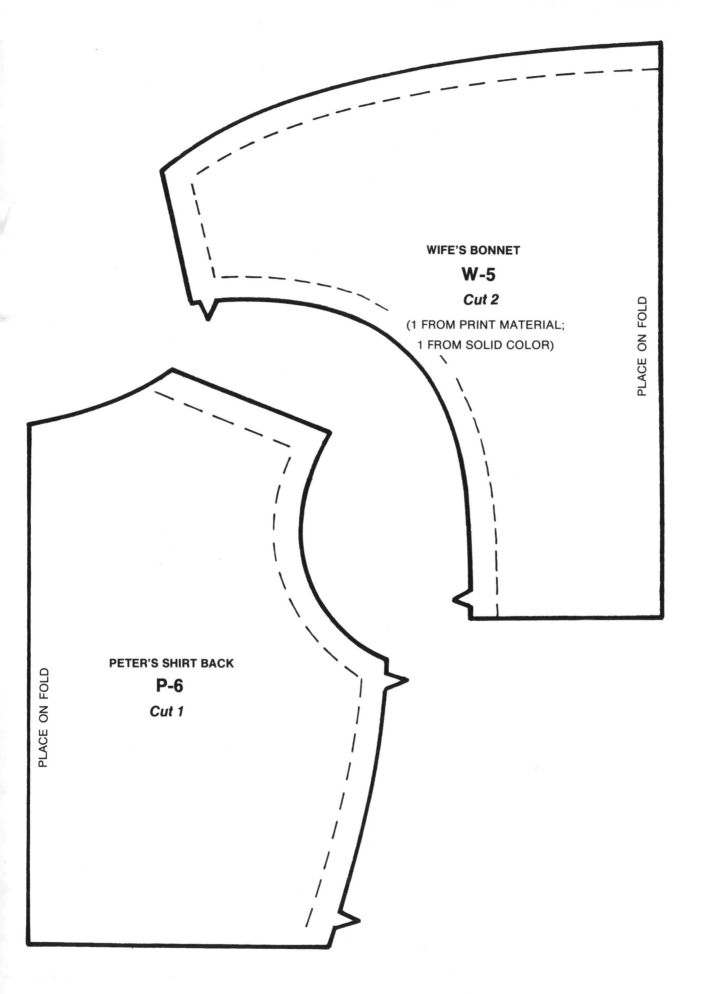

WIFE'S BONNET

W-5

Cut 2

(1 FROM PRINT MATERIAL;
1 FROM SOLID COLOR)

PLACE ON FOLD

PETER'S SHIRT BACK

P-6

Cut 1

PLACE ON FOLD

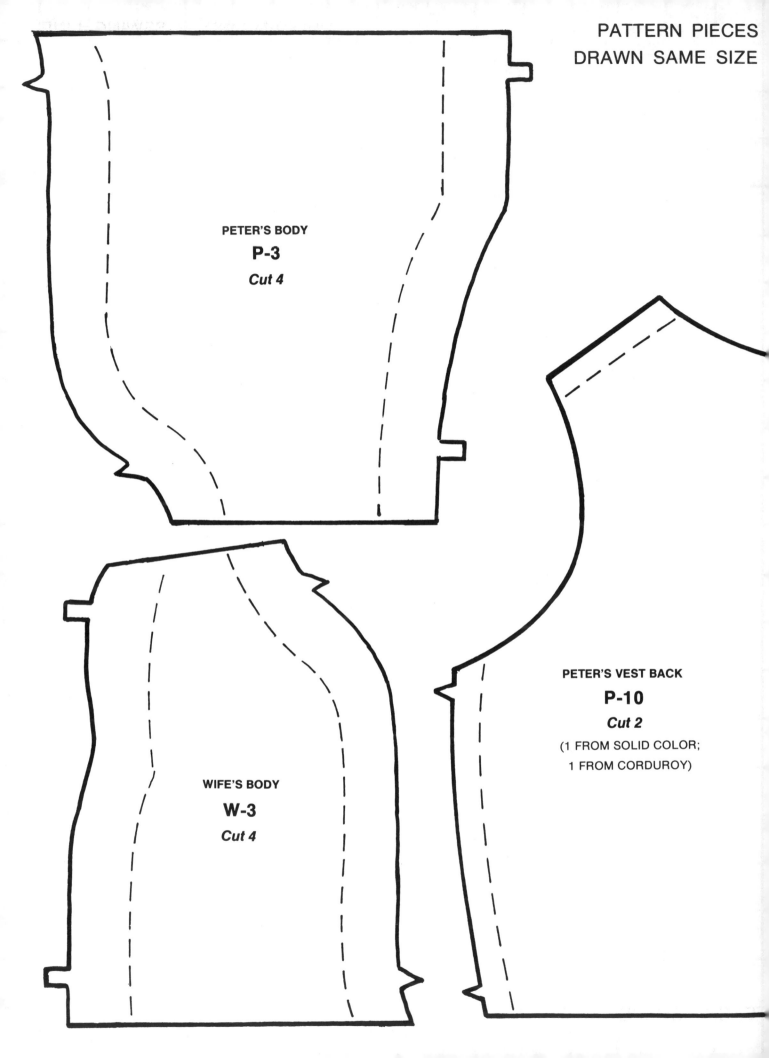

PATTERN PIECES
DRAWN SAME SIZE

PETER'S BODY
P-3
Cut 4

WIFE'S BODY
W-3
Cut 4

PETER'S VEST BACK
P-10
Cut 2
(1 FROM SOLID COLOR;
1 FROM CORDUROY)

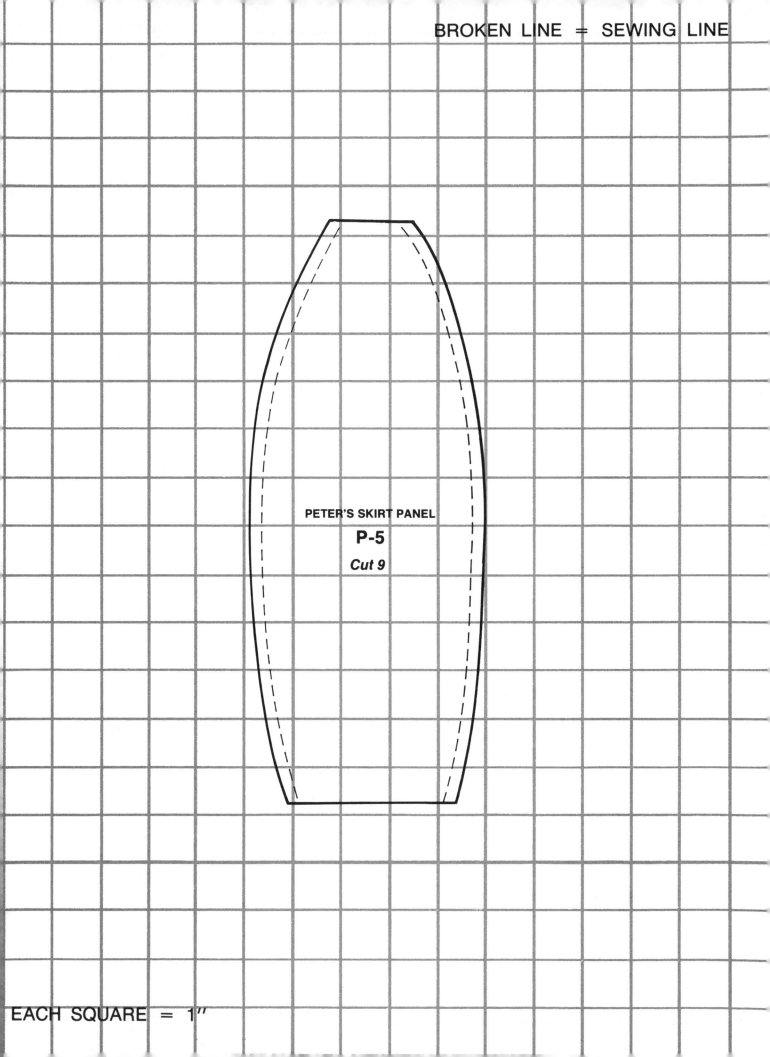

BROKEN LINE = SEWING LINE

PETER'S SKIRT PANEL

P-5

Cut 9

EACH SQUARE = 1"

SEWING AND EMBROIDERING

Peter's head-and-body:

With right sides facing, pin and baste the two face sections (P-1) together only on the side with the nose and mouth. Remove pins and machine-stitch down this side. Then take the two head-back sections (P-2) and, again with right sides facing, pin and baste them together only on the side *without* notches. Remove pins and machine-stitch down this side. Match the notches of the face piece with those of the head-back piece and pin these sides together, right sides facing. (Fig. 1). Baste, remove pins and machine-stitch.

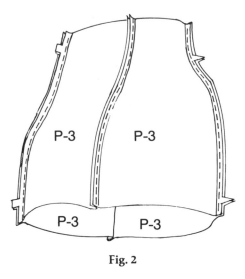

Fig. 2

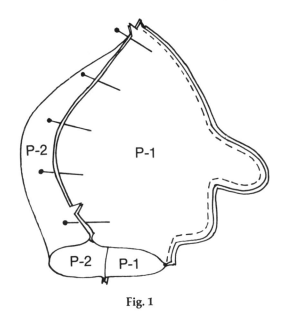

Fig. 1

Next take the four body sections (P-3) and, with right sides facing, match the square notches of one section with the square notches of another, the triangular notches with the triangular notches, and so on. Pin and baste these sides together, then remove pins and machine-stitch. (Fig. 2).

Now, again with right sides facing, baste and machine-stitch the head to the body at the neck, leaving ½" (1.25 cm.) seam. Remove all basting thread. Trim the seams and clip the curves. Turn the material right side out and stuff with polyester fiberfill, packing it until the head-and-body is very, very stiff.

Hand-stitch the opening with heavy-duty thread, using a whip stitch.

Peter's arms:

Match the notches and baste two arm sections (P-4) together, right sides facing. Machine-stitch where indicated on the pattern, leaving the bottom opening for stuffing. Remove basting thread. Repeat this procedure with the other arm. Trim the seams and clip the corners. Turn the material right side out and stuff as above. Hand-stitch the hands to make fingers as shown in illustration. (Fig. 3). Then turn in the opening and whip-stitch the arms to the body with heavy-duty thread.

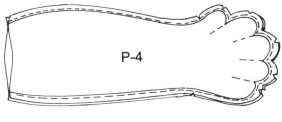

Fig. 3

Peter's face:

Using the face drawing (Fig. 4) as a guide, draw Peter's face with a pencil onto the stuffed head. Then embroider the features with a single strand of embroidery floss. Use

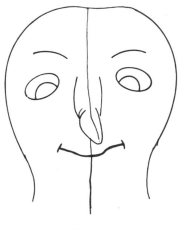

Fig. 4

black for the mouth, eyes and eyebrows, working in an outline stitch. Use dark blue for the iris and work in a satin stitch. Shape the nose by hand-stitching from one side to the other. This should make a line where the nose juts out from the cheeks.

Wife's head-and-body:

With right sides facing, pin and baste the two face sections (W-1) together only on the side with the nose and mouth. Remove pins and machine-stitch down this side. Then take the two head-back sections (W-2) and, again with right sides facing, pin and baste them together only on the side *without* notches. Remove pins and machine-stitch down this side. Match the notches of the face piece with those of the head-back piece and pin these sides together, right sides facing. (See Fig. 1). Baste, remove pins, and machine-stitch.

Next, take the four body sections (W-3) and, with right sides facing, match the square notches of one section with the square notches of another, the triangular notches with the triangular notches and so on. Pin and baste these sides together, then remove pins and machine stitch. (See Fig. 2).

Now, again with right sides facing, baste and machine-stitch the head to the body at the neck, leaving a ½" (1.25 cm.) seam. Remove all basting thread. Trim the seams and clip the curves. Turn the material right side out and stuff with polyester fiberfill, packing it until the head-and-body is very,

very stiff. Hand-stitch the opening with heavy-duty thread, using a whip stitch.

Wife's arms:

Match the notches and baste two arm sections (W-4) together, right sides facing. Machine-stitch where indicated on the pattern, leaving the bottom open for stuffing. Remove basting thread. Repeat this procedure with the other arm. Trim the seams and clip the corners. Turn the material right side out and stuff as above. Hand-stitch the hands to make fingers as shown in illustration. (See Fig. 3). Then turn in the opening and whip-stitch the arms to the body with heavy-duty thread.

Wife's face:

Using the face drawing (Fig. 5) as a guide, draw the wife's face with a pencil onto the stuffed head. Then embroider the features

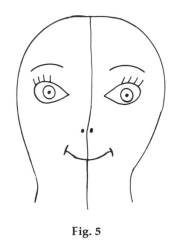

Fig. 5

with a single strand of embroidery floss. Use red for the nose and mouth, working in an outline stitch. Use black for the eyes, eyebrows and eyelashes. The eyes and eyebrows are worked in an outline stitch, the eyelashes in a straight stitch. Use light blue for the iris and work in a buttonhole stitch. Make a black French knot in the center for the pupils. Shape the nose by hand-stitching from one side to the other. This should make a line where the nose juts out from the cheeks.

DOLL ASSEMBLY

When attaching the two parts together, turn Peter in the same direction as his wife. (Fig. 6). Using heavy-duty thread and the whip stitch, hand-stitch Peter to his wife firmly at the waist so that the doll does not bend.

Fig. 7

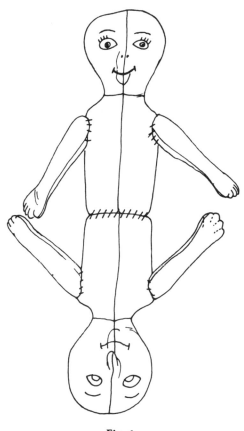

Fig. 6

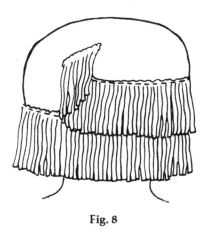

Fig. 8

rows of yarn. (Fig. 8). Then place the third piece of the yarn at the crown of the head, the stitched edge doubled and forming a part. (Fig. 9).

HAIR

Peter:

Make three 2 x 6″ (5 x 15 cm.) pieces of cardboard and wind brown yarn approximately 40 times around each piece, looping around the 2″ (5 cm.) side. Then machine-stitch along one 6″ (15 cm.) end—at ¼″ (6 mm.) from the edge—and cut the loops at the other end of the yarn with scissors. (Fig. 7). Remove all the cardboard.

Next, starting at the bottom and at the back of Peter's head, arrange and stitch two

Fig. 9

Wife:

Wrap brown yarn 10 times around a pencil, slip it off, and hand-stitch it to the wife's forehead as shown in illustration. (Fig. 10). Then take an 8 x 3″ (20 x 7.5 cm.) piece

Fig. 10

of cardboard and wind yarn approximately 50 times around it, looping around the 8″ (20 cm.) side. Cut the loops at one end and remove the cardboard. Stretch out the yarn to its 16″ (40 cm.) length. Now machine-stitch across the middle, forming a part. You should have 8″ (20 cm.) on either side of the part. Place the yarn on the wife's head, and hand-stitch all the way down the part to secure. Frame the hair around the face, and hand-stitch against the head, 1″ (2.5 cm.) on either side of the part. Now take all the excess yarn and roll it into a bun, stitching here and there to secure. (Fig. 11).

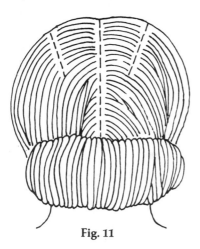

Fig. 11

MAKING THE CLOTHES

Peter's shirt:

Baste and machine-stitch the back (P-6) to the two sections of the front (P-7) at the shoulders, right sides facing. Then hem down both sections of the front. Next take the two sections of the collar (P-8) and, with right sides facing, baste and machine-stitch them together where marked on the pattern. Clip the curves, remove basting thread and turn the collar right side out.

Turn under one raw edge of the collar and baste it to the right side of the shirt neck. Clip the curves. Then turn under the other raw edge of the collar and baste it to the other side of the shirt neck, as shown in illustration. (Fig. 12). Top-stitch across the basted edge and around the other edges of the collar.

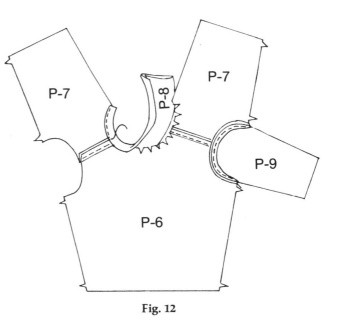

Fig. 12

Now take the sleeves (P-9) and hem along the straight edge. Then baste and machine-stitch the sleeves to the shirt, the curved edge set at the armhole. (See Fig. 12). Now baste and machine-stitch down the sleeves, and, with notches matching, down the sides of the shirt. Remove all basting thread. Sew on two buttons to the shirt front, and slip-stitch the shirt onto Peter.

Peter's vest:

Take the vest back (P-10) and, with right sides facing, baste and machine-stitch the lining to the corduroy at the armholes and around the neck. Then do the same with the front sections (P-11) and this time also machine-stitch all the way down the front. Clip the corners and turn material right side out. Top-stitch around the armholes, around the neck and down the front.

Next, with right sides facing, baste and machine-stitch the back to the front pieces at the shoulders, and, with notches matching, down the sides. Hem the bottom ½" (1.25 cm.). Turn vest right side out. Put aside.

Peter's and Wife's skirts:

The skirts for Peter and his wife are made together. First baste and machine-stitch the nine skirt panel sections (P-5) together. (Fig. 13). This piece should now measure 27" (67.5

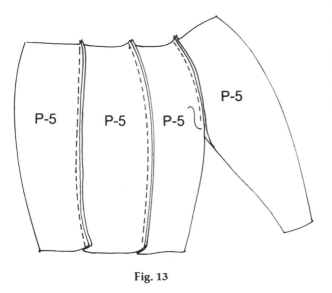

Fig. 13

cm.) on one side and approximately 11" (27.5 cm.) on the other side. Remove basting thread. Then take the 36 x 12" (90 x 30 cm.) cotton print material and machine-stitch gathering stitches on both the 36" (90 cm.) edges. Pull only one edge to 27" (67.5 cm.); leave the other edge as it is for the moment.

Now, with right sides facing, pin the

cotton print material to the felt piece along the 27" (67.5 cm.) edge. This will now be the hemline. Leave a ¼" (6 mm.) seam and baste and machine-stitch the sections together along the hemline. (Fig. 14).

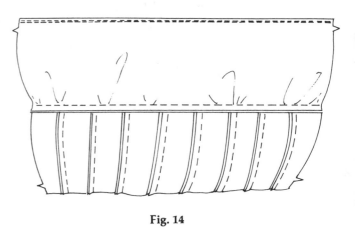

Fig. 14

Fold the fabric in half with the right sides facing so that the piece now measures 23½" (58.75 cm.) from top to bottom, and 13½" (33.75 cm.) across the middle. Baste along the 23½" (58.75 cm.) edge. (The previously stitched seam now faces itself.) Measure 2" (5 cm.) in from each end—along basted edge—and mark with pins. (Fig. 15). Machine-stitch between these pin marks, back-stitching at the beginning and end to secure the seam. Remove pins and basting thread.

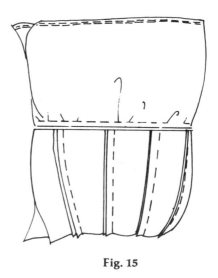

Fig. 15

Now turn this tubular piece inside out, wrong sides facing, and match the top raw edges as shown in illustration. (Fig. 16). Top-stitch along the hemline. The raw edges become the skirt waistlines. The seams become the center backs of the skirts.

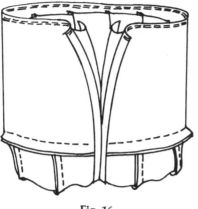

Fig. 16

Peter's and Wife's waistbands:

With right sides facing, fold the cotton print waistband strip—11 x 1¾" (27.5 x 4.5 cm.)—in half lengthwise and machine-stitch each end. Back-stitch to make them secure. Next, turn the piece to the right side and press. Pull to shape the top raw edge of the cotton print skirt to fit the waistband. Turn under one right side raw edge of the band and pin to the right side top raw edge of this skirt, matching each end with the center-back seam of the skirt. Baste, remove pins and machine-stitch. Remove basting thread.

Flip the waistband over the top of the skirt and, turning under the remaining raw edge of the band, hemstitch it to the other side to encase the top raw edge of the same skirt. (Fig. 17). Repeat this procedure with the other

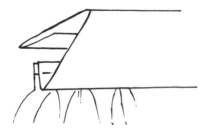

Fig. 17

waistband to encase the top raw edge of the orange felt skirt. However, in this case you don't need to gather the skirt as it will be narrow enough at the top. Use the solid cotton material for this waistband. Put aside.

Wife's bonnet:

Take the two sections of the brim (W-6), the print material and the solid color lining. Now, with right sides facing, baste and machine-stitch them together around the outer edge. Clip the curves and turn the brim right side out. Then place the brim—the side with the seam line on the pattern—around the right side top edge of the print section of the bonnet (W-5) with print side of the brim facing it. (Fig. 18). (You will have to stretch out the curve.) Baste them together.

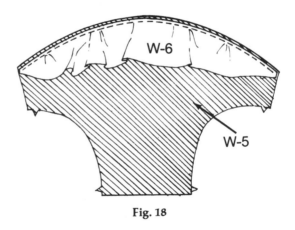

Fig. 18

Now place the solid color section of the bonnet over this with the right side facing the brim and the print bonnet section. (Fig. 19).

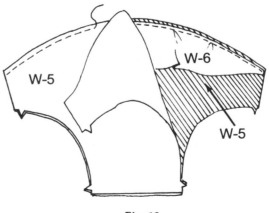

Fig. 19

Now baste and machine-stitch all around, but leave the straight edge open for turning. Remove basting thread and clip the curves. Turn bonnet right side out. Fold under the opening and top-stitch.

Then take the two 12 x 1″ (30 x 2.5 cm.) strips, hem all the edges and machine-stitch them to the inside of the bonnet at the wings. Now match the notches (see Fig. 19), the upper left side notch with the lower left side notch. Do the same with the right side. Sew tightly at the point where the notches meet, and add two small buttons. Put aside.

Wife's blouse:

Stretch out the blouse material (W-7), then cut the back as shown in illustration. (Fig. 20). Hem the back where you have just

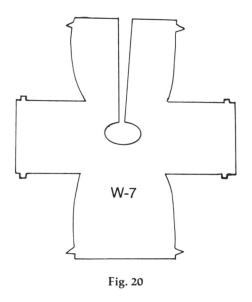

Fig. 20

cut it. Hem the neck, and the sleeves at the cuffs. (The sections with square notches are sleeves.) Now fold the blouse, matching square notches with square notches, and triangular notches with triangular notches. (Fig. 21). Baste and machine-stitch along the sleeves and down the sides. Remove basting

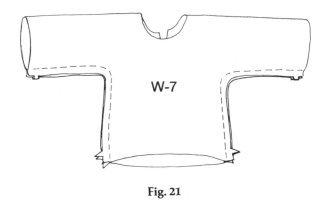

Fig. 21

thread. Add elastic to the sleeve ½″ (1.25 cm.) from the cuffs. Put the blouse on the doll and hemstitch the back closed. Make folds and stitch blouse to doll.

Wife's apron:

The top and bottom are 9″ (22.5 cm.) and the sides are 16″ (40 cm.). Hem the apron 1″ (2.5 cm.) at the bottom and ¼″ (6 mm.) on the sides. Then gather the top of the apron and pull until it measures 5″ (12.5 cm.). Now take the 5 x 1″ (12.5 x 2.5 cm.) strip and fold it in half lengthwise. Turn under the raw edges and encase the gathered edge of the apron with it. Baste and machine-stitch. Remove basting thread. Finally, take the two 11 x ½″ (27.5 x 1.25 cm.) strips, hem all the edges and machine-stitch to apron band. Put aside.

FINISHING

Put the skirt on Peter. The seam should be at the back. Hand-stitch the waistband to the doll and hand-stitch the skirt's seam closed. Put the vest on, hand-stitch a button into place at the top and slip-stitch the vest closed. Turn the doll upside down and hand-stitch the over waistband to his wife. Hand-stitch the skirt's seam closed. Tie on the bonnet and the apron.

Alice, the Mad Hatter
and the March Hare

THUS GREW THE TALE of Wonderland:
  Thus slowly, one by one,
Its quaint events were hammered out—
  And now the tale is done,
And home we steer, a merry crew,
  Beneath the setting sun.

Alice, the Mad Hatter and the March Hare

MATERIALS YOU'LL NEED

½ yard (45 cm.) light pink cotton material—Alice and the Mad Hatter's head-and-body, lining for March Hare's ears (A-1, A-2, H-1, M-3)

¼ yard (22.5 cm.) white terry cloth—March Hare's head-and-body (M-1, M-2, M-3, M-4)

½ yard (45 cm.) cotton print material—Alice's blouse and skirt (A-3, A-4, A-5)

½ yard (45 cm.) solid color cotton material—Mad Hatter and March Hare's skirt

⅓ yard (30 cm.) white cotton material—Alice's apron and Mad Hatter's shirt (A-6, A-7, H-13, H-14)

A 9 x 12″ (22.5 x 30 cm.) piece of black felt—Mad Hatter's eyes, March Hare's jacket, and parts of the Mad Hatter's outfit (H-2, H-6, H-8, H-9, H-10, H-11)

¼ yard (22.5 cm.) red felt—Mad Hatter's hat and jacket, Queen of Hearts (H-3, H-4, H-5, H-9, H-10, H-11, Q-1)

Scraps of gold and green felt—Mad Hatter's feathers (H-7)

A scrap of pink felt—March Hare's eyes, nose and bow tie (M-5, M-6, M-8)

Scraps of white and orange felt—Queen of Hearts' face and crown (Q-2, Q-3)

A 9 x 12″ piece of light blue felt—March Hare's vest (M-7)

A 4 x 4″ (10 x 10 cm.) piece of matching print cotton material—Mad Hatter's bow tie (H-12)

4-ounce skein of yellow yarn—Alice's hair

2-ounce skein of black yarn—Mad Hatter's hair

1 yard (90 cm.) white medium-width lace—Alice's skirt, blouse and apron

2 small white buttons

1 snap

Black, blue, pink, and red embroidery floss for faces

Sewing thread and heavy-duty thread to match materials

1½ pounds of polyester fiberfill for stuffing

Note: All seam allowances are ½″ (1.25 cm.) for dolls, and ¼″ (6 mm.) for clothes.

CUTTING

Alice's head-and-body and clothes:

Make the paper patterns from the pattern pieces (A-1 through A-7), enlarging, if needed, to actual size. Cut all pattern pieces from material, remembering to reverse the pattern when pairs are needed.

For Alice's skirt, cut a rectangle 36 x 12″ (90 x 30 cm.), and a strip 10 x 1¾″ (25 x 4.5 cm.) for the waistband.

For Alice's blouse, cut two strips 5 x 1″ (12.5 x 2.5 cm.) for the cuffs. For Alice's apron, cut a strip 19 x 2″ (47.5 x 5 cm.) for the tie.

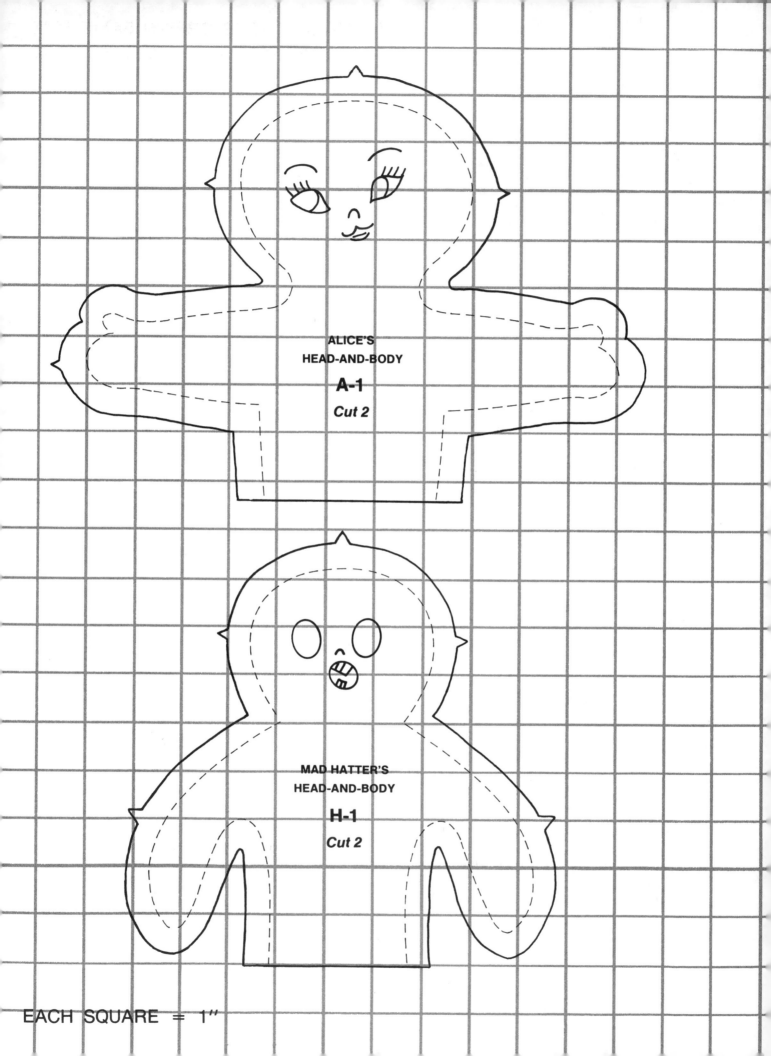

ALICE'S
HEAD-AND-BODY

A-1

Cut 2

MAD HATTER'S
HEAD-AND-BODY

H-1

Cut 2

EACH SQUARE = 1"

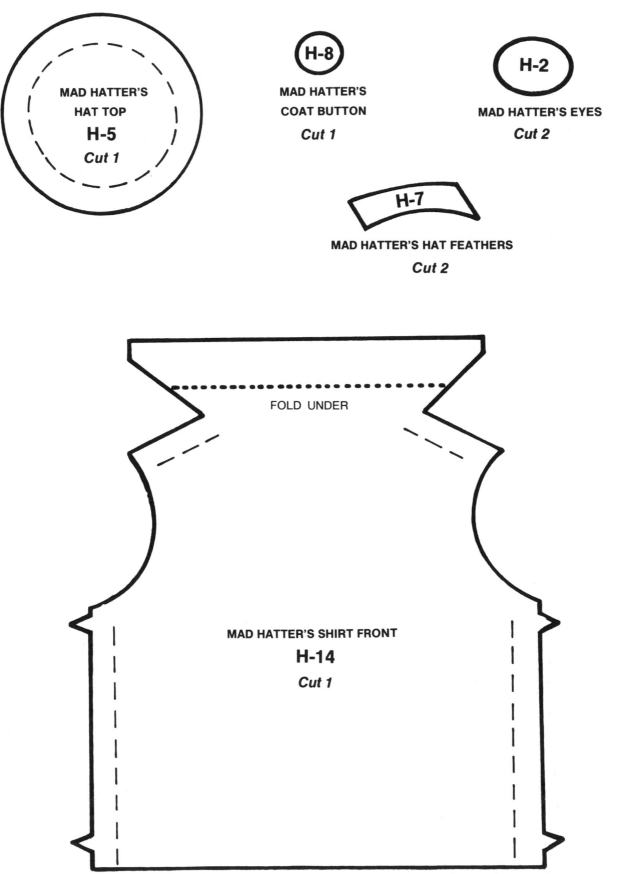

MAD HATTER'S
HAT TOP
H-5
Cut 1

H-8

MAD HATTER'S
COAT BUTTON
Cut 1

H-2

MAD HATTER'S EYES
Cut 2

H-7

MAD HATTER'S HAT FEATHERS
Cut 2

FOLD UNDER

MAD HATTER'S SHIRT FRONT
H-14
Cut 1

PATTERN PIECES DRAWN SAME SIZE

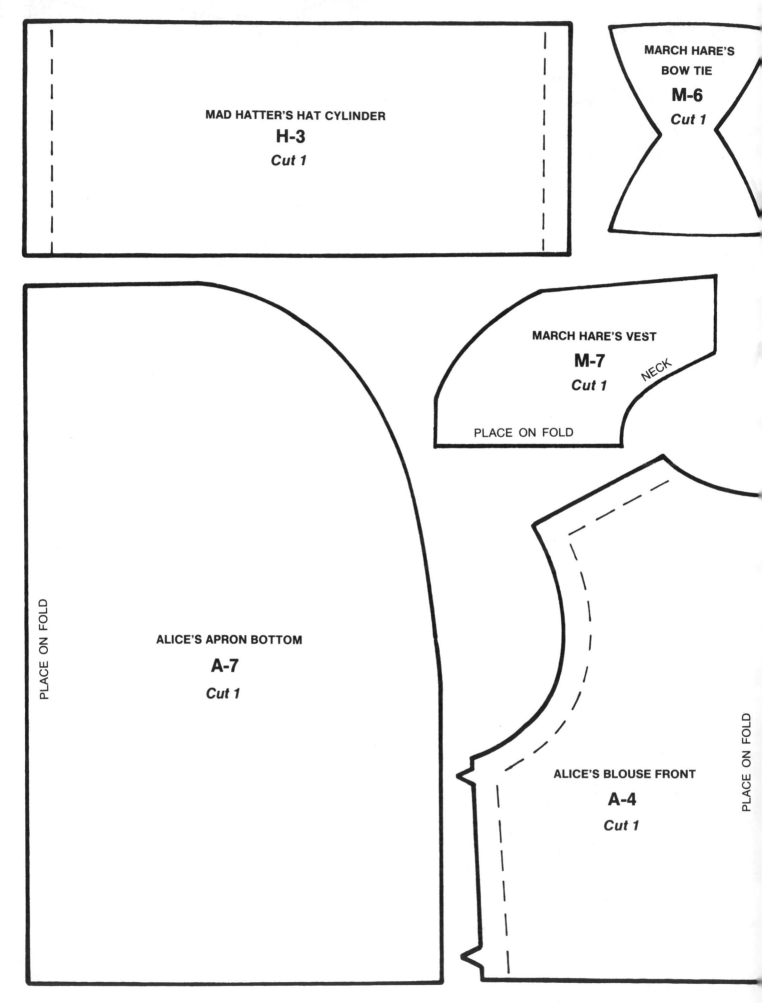

MAD HATTER'S HAT CYLINDER
H-3
Cut 1

MARCH HARE'S
BOW TIE
M-6
Cut 1

MARCH HARE'S VEST
M-7
Cut 1

NECK

PLACE ON FOLD

PLACE ON FOLD

ALICE'S APRON BOTTOM
A-7
Cut 1

ALICE'S BLOUSE FRONT
A-4
Cut 1

PLACE ON FOLD

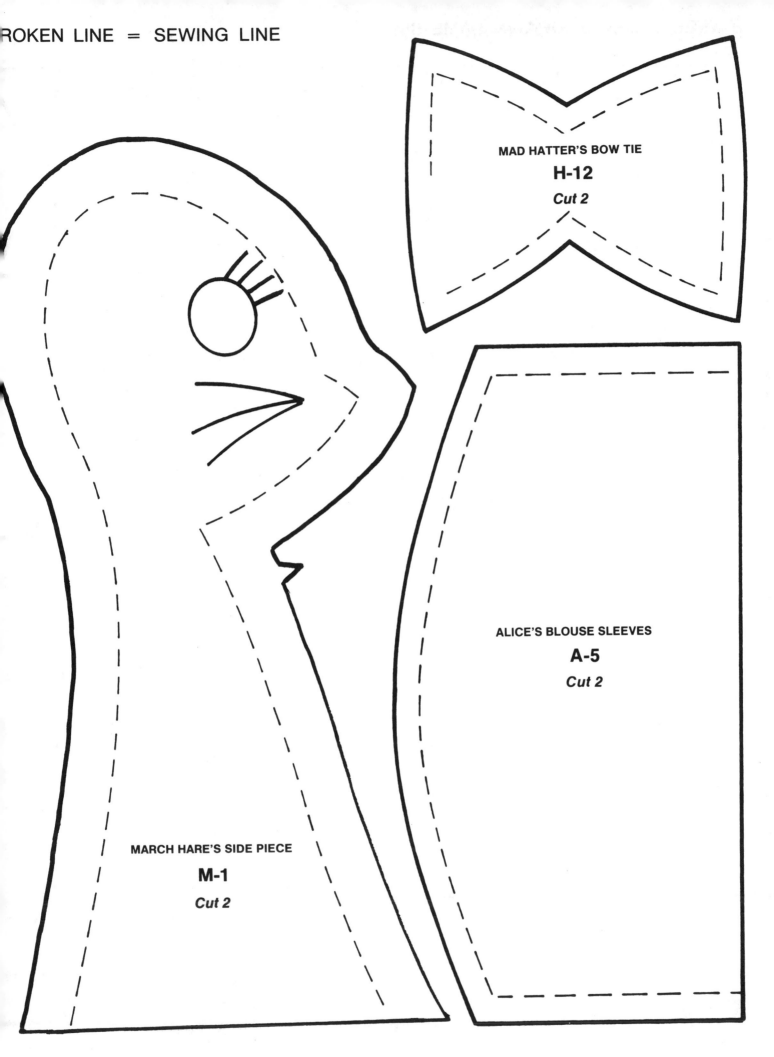

BROKEN LINE = SEWING LINE

MAD HATTER'S BOW TIE

H-12

Cut 2

ALICE'S BLOUSE SLEEVES

A-5

Cut 2

MARCH HARE'S SIDE PIECE

M-1

Cut 2

PATTERN PIECES DRAWN SAME SIZE

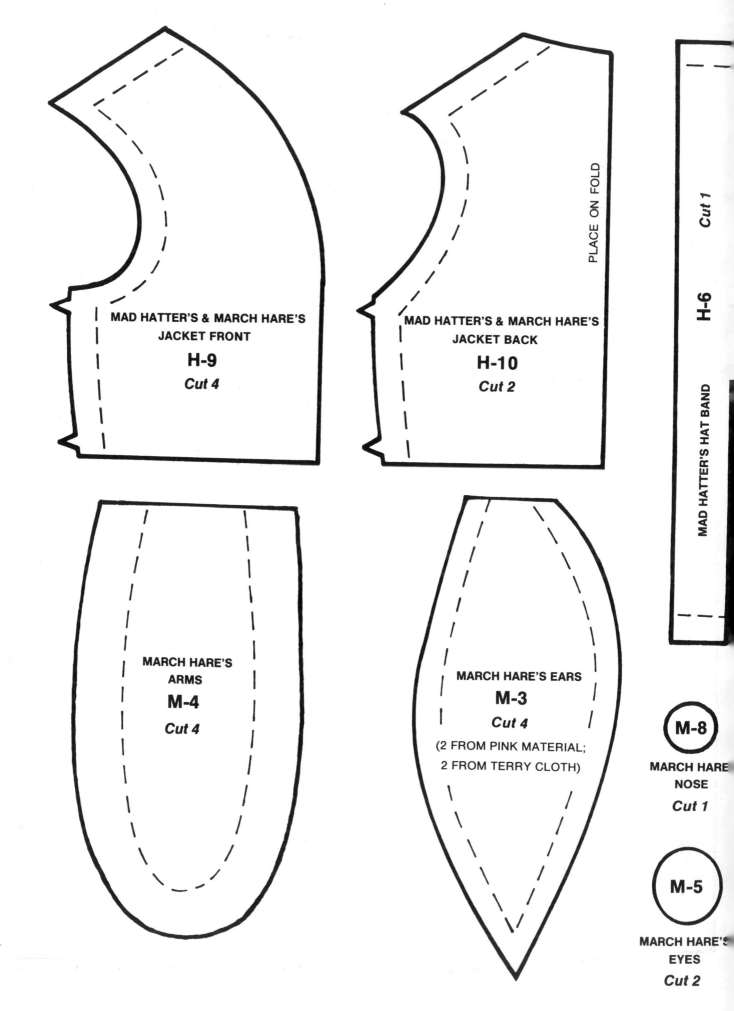

MAD HATTER'S & MARCH HARE'S
JACKET FRONT

H-9

Cut 4

MAD HATTER'S & MARCH HARE'S
JACKET BACK

H-10

Cut 2

PLACE ON FOLD

H-6

Cut 1

MAD HATTER'S HAT BAND

MARCH HARE'S
ARMS

M-4

Cut 4

MARCH HARE'S EARS

M-3

Cut 4

(2 FROM PINK MATERIAL;
2 FROM TERRY CLOTH)

M-8

MARCH HARE'S
NOSE

Cut 1

M-5

MARCH HARE'S
EYES

Cut 2

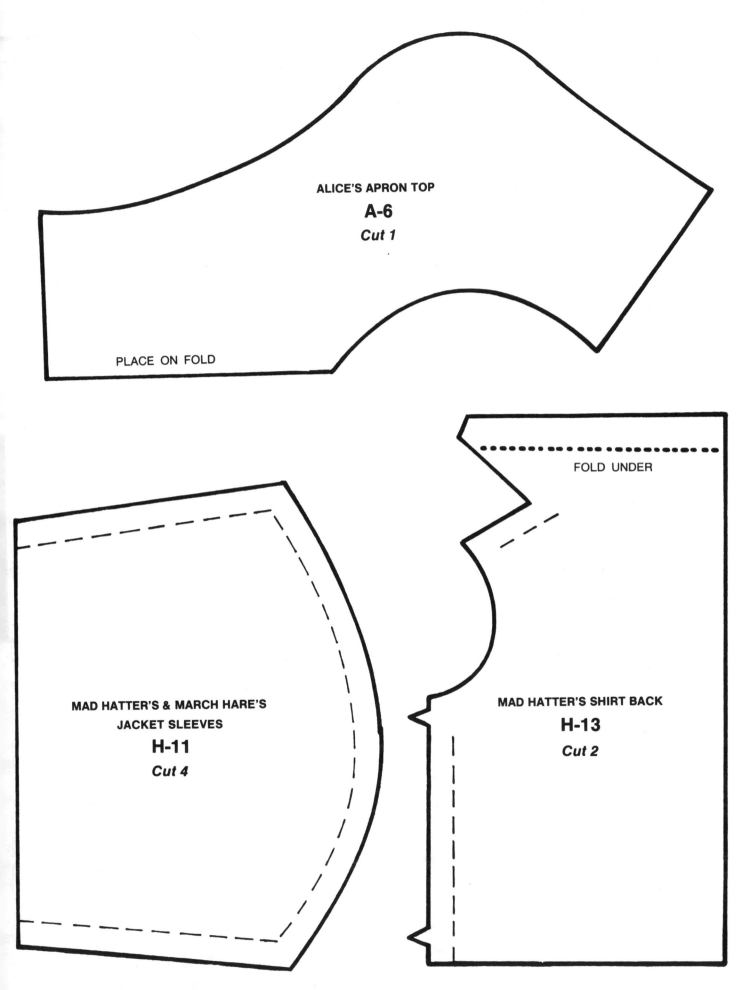

BROKEN LINE = SEWING LINE

ALICE'S APRON TOP
A-6
Cut 1

PLACE ON FOLD

FOLD UNDER

MAD HATTER'S & MARCH HARE'S
JACKET SLEEVES
H-11
Cut 4

MAD HATTER'S SHIRT BACK
H-13
Cut 2

PATTERN PIECES DRAWN SAME SIZE

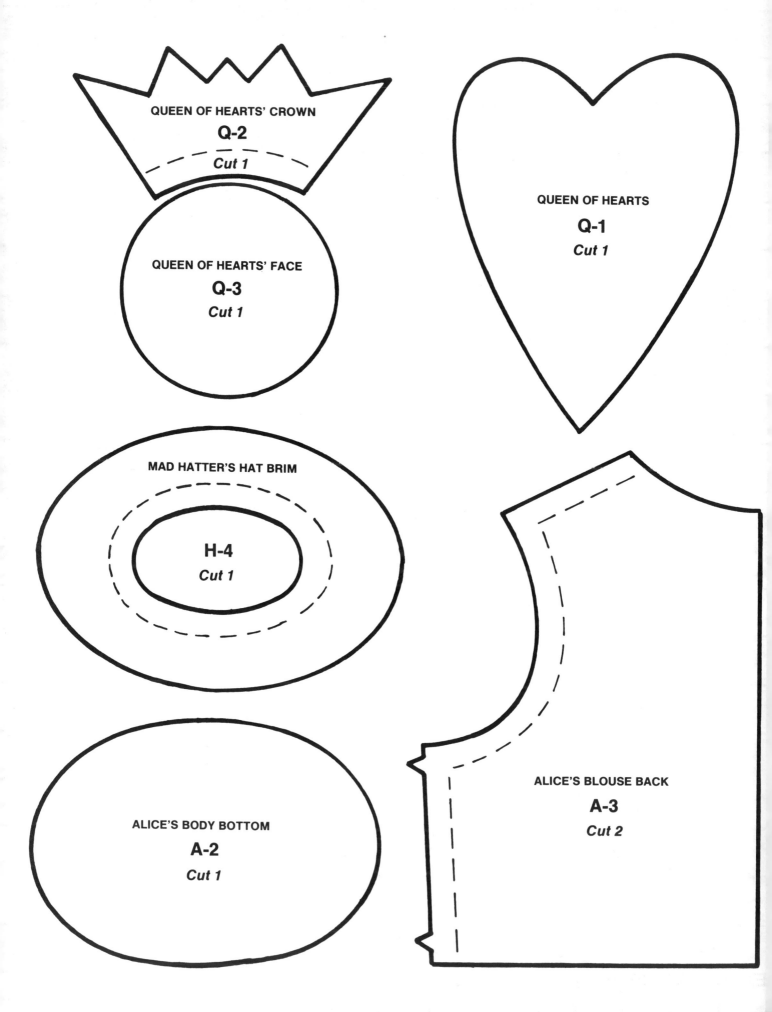

QUEEN OF HEARTS' CROWN

Q-2

Cut 1

QUEEN OF HEARTS

Q-1

Cut 1

QUEEN OF HEARTS' FACE

Q-3

Cut 1

MAD HATTER'S HAT BRIM

H-4

Cut 1

ALICE'S BLOUSE BACK

A-3

Cut 2

ALICE'S BODY BOTTOM

A-2

Cut 1

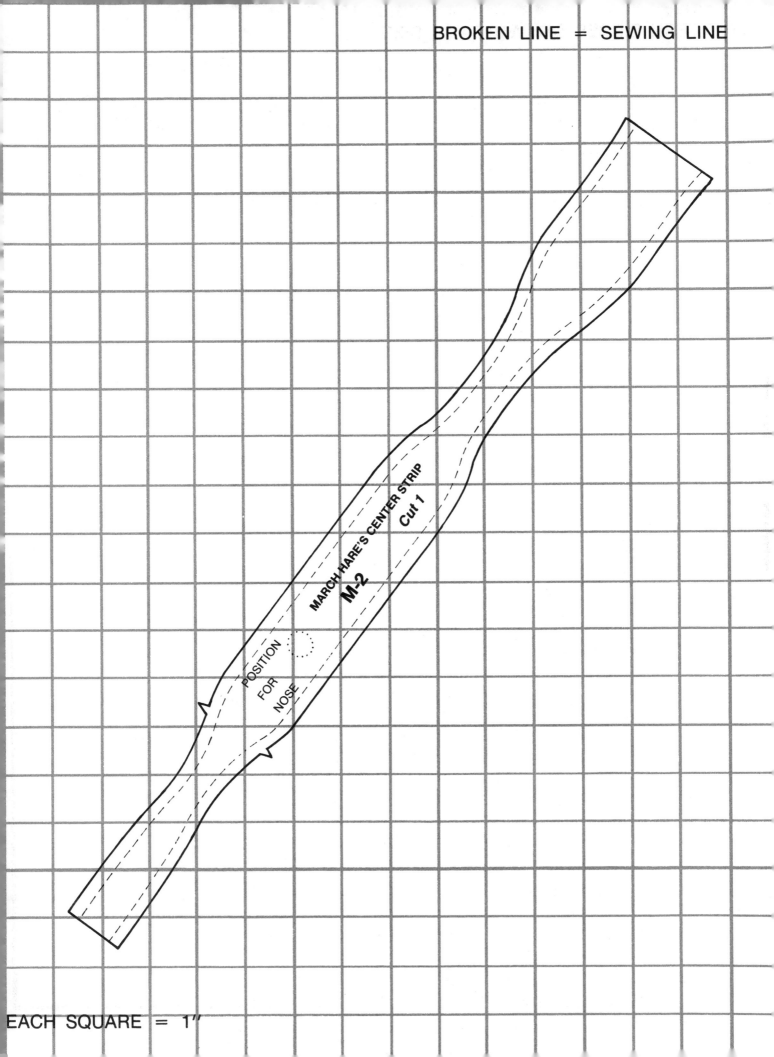

BROKEN LINE = SEWING LINE

MARCH HARE'S CENTER STRIP
M-2
Cut 1

POSITION
FOR
NOSE

EACH SQUARE = 1"

Mad Hatter's and March Hare's head-and-body and clothes:

Make the paper patterns from the pattern pieces (H-1 through H-14 and M-1 through M-8) enlarging, if needed, to actual size. Cut all pattern pieces from material, remembering to reverse the pattern when pairs are needed. For the March Hare's ears (M-3), cut two from terry cloth and two from pink cotton.

For the Mad Hatter's and the March Hare's skirt, cut a rectangle 36 x 12″ (90 x 30 cm.), and a strip 12 x 1¾″ (30 x 4.5 cm.) for the waistband.

SEWING AND EMBROIDERING

Alice's face:

Using the face drawing (Fig. 1) as a guide, draw Alice's face with a pencil onto one of the head-and-body sections. Then, using an

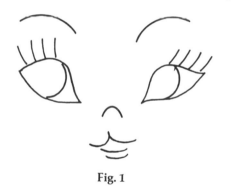

Fig. 1

embroidery hoop, embroider the features with a single strand of embroidery floss. Use red for the nose and mouth, working in an outline stitch. Use black for the eyes, eyebrows and eyelashes. The eyes and eyebrows are worked in an outline stitch, the eyelashes in a straight stitch. Use blue for the iris and work in a satin stitch.

Alice's head-and-body:

Match the notches and baste the head-and-body sections (A-1) together, right sides facing. Machine-stitch where indicated on the pattern, leaving the bottom open for stuffing. Remove basting thread. Trim the seams and

clip the curves as illustrated. (Fig. 2). Turn the material right side out and stuff with polyester fiberfill, packing it until the body is very, very stiff. Then hand-stitch the bottom piece (A-2) to the head-and-body with heavy duty thread, using a whip stitch.

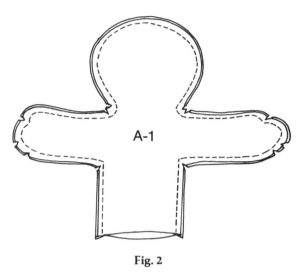

Fig. 2

Mad Hatter's face:

Using the face drawing (Fig. 3) as a guide, draw the Mad Hatter's face with a pencil onto one of the head-and-body sections. Then,

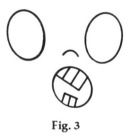

Fig. 3

using an embroidery hoop, embroider the features with a single strand of embroidery floss. Use red for the mouth, working in an outline stitch. Use black for the teeth and nose. The teeth are worked in a straight stitch and an outline stitch. The nose is worked in a straight stitch, slanted up and down. Top-stitch the felt eyes (H-2) in place.

Mad Hatter's head-and-body:

Match the notches and baste the head-and-body sections (H-1) together, right sides facing. Machine-stitch where indicated on the pattern, leaving the bottom open for stuffing. Remove basting thread. Trim the seams and clip the curves. Turn the material right side out and stuff with polyester fiberfill, packing it until the body is very, very stiff. Then hand-stitch the opening with heavy-duty thread, using a whip stitch.

March Hare's head-and-body:

Take one of March Hare's side pieces (M-1) and ease the March Hare's center strip (M-2) around it. (Fig. 4). Pin and baste these

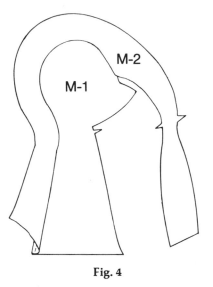

Fig. 4

together. Make sure the notch on the side piece matches with the notch on the center strip. Then remove pins and machine-stitch. Add the second side piece to the other side of the center strip in the same way.

Trim the seams and clip the curves. Remove all basting thread. Turn the material right side out and stuff with polyester fiberfill, packing it until the body is very, very stiff. Hand-stitch the opening with heavy-duty thread, using a whip stitch.

March Hare's arms:

Match the notches and baste two arm sections (M-4) together, right sides facing. Machine-stitch where indicated on the pattern, leaving the bottom open for stuffing.

Remove basting thread. Trim the seams and clip the curves. Make the second arm in the same way. Turn the material right side out and stuff as above. Turn in the opening and hand-stitch the opening closed. Then hand-stitch the arms to the body as shown in illustration. (Fig. 5).

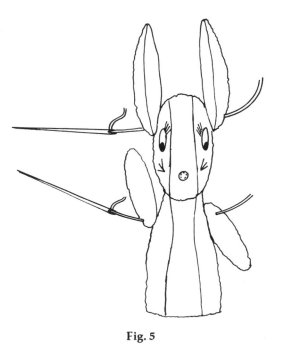

Fig. 5

March Hare's ears:

Take two ear sections (M-3) , one of terry cloth and one of the lining material. With right sides facing, baste and machine-stitch these two sections together where indicated on the pattern. Remove basting thread. Trim the seams and clip the curves. Make the second ear in the same way. Then turn the ears right side out, stuff lightly with polyester fiberfill and hand-stitch the opening closed. Then hand-stitch the ears in place, as shown in illustration. (See Fig. 5).

March Hare's face:

Stitch a tiny piece of black felt onto the pink felt eyes (M-5). Then stitch the eyes in place as shown in illustration. (Fig. 6). Then draw the eyebrows and whiskers with a pencil, and embroider them with black floss, using a straight stitch. Finally, stitch the nose

Fig. 6

(M-8) in place. It should be at the tip of the muzzle, (see dotted line on pattern).

DOLL ASSEMBLY

When attaching the three parts together, first hand-stitch the Mad Hatter and the March Hare at the bottom, using heavy-duty

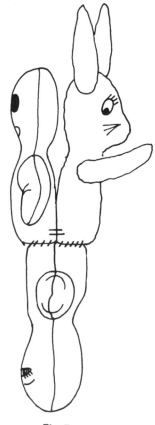

Fig. 7

thread. Then face the Mad Hatter in the same direction as Alice. Using the whip stitch join them firmly at the waist so that the doll does not bend (Fig. 7).

HAIR

Alice's hair:

To make the bangs wrap yellow yarn 15 times around the middle three fingers, tie one end and cut the other end. Stitch the tied end to the back of Alice's head about 1″ (2.5 cm.) below the top seam line. Stretch the yarn down her forehead and with a needle and yellow thread stitch across to form the bangs. (Fig. 8).

Fig. 8

Now wind some more yellow yarn 70 times around an 8 x 6″ (20 x 15 cm.) piece of cardboard, looping around the 8″ (20 cm.) side. Then tie the loops at one end with yarn as shown in illustration (Fig. 9), and cut the

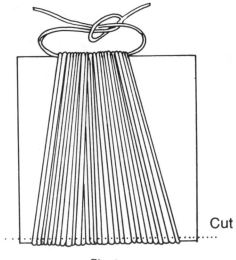

Cut

Fig. 9

other end. Place the tied part at the crown of the head and hand-stitch with yellow thread to secure and also to form a ½" (1.25 cm.) part. Remove the tie and arrange the loose yarn, framing it around the face and giving a little fullness at the back. Then stitch across the base of the head, using yellow yarn. (Fig. 10).

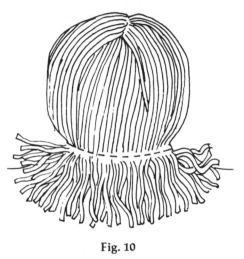

Fig. 10

Mad Hatter's hair:

Wind black yarn 40 times around a 3½ x 3½" (8.75 x 8.75 cm.) piece of cardboard. Tie the loops at one end with yarn, and cut the other end. Place the tied part at the top of the Mad Hatter's head and arrange the loose yarn around the head. Stitch at the top to secure. Then, with a needle and black yarn stitch across the back of the head as shown in illustration. (Fig. 11).

Fig. 11

MAKING THE CLOTHES

Alice's blouse:

Baste and machine-stitch the two sections of the back (A-3) to the front (A-4) at the shoulders, right sides facing. Now cut a strip on the bias from the same print material to fit the neck. The strip should be about ½" (1.25 cm.) wide. Fold this strip in half lengthwise, turn under the raw edges and encase the neck of the blouse. (Fig. 12). Insert lace in between, baste and top-stitch.

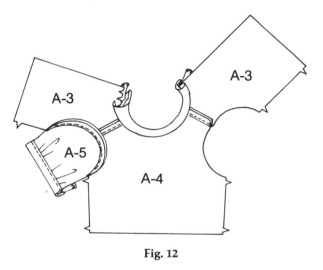

Fig. 12

Take the sleeves (A-5) and gather the straight edge to 5" (12.5 cm.). Then fold the 5 x 1" (12.5 x 2.5 cm.) strip in half lengthwise, turn under the raw edges and, slipping some lace in between, encase the gathered edge of the sleeves. (Fig. 13). Baste and top-stitch. Set the sleeves into the armholes, baste and

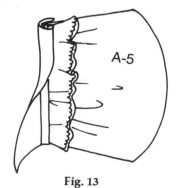

Fig. 13

machine-stitch. Then baste and machine-stitch down the sides of the sleeves, right sides facing.

Finally, match the notches of the back sections to the notches of the front and baste and machine-stitch down the sides. Remove all basting thread. Fit the blouse on Alice, turn under one raw edge of the back, place it over the other and hemstitch it closed.

Apron:

Hem all the edges of the apron top (A-6) except the bottom straight edge. Add lace to the outer edges by machine-stitching. Then hem the bottom (A-7) around the curved edges and add white lace by machine-stitching. Gather the straight edge of the bottom to fit the top. With right sides facing, match the raw edges of the apron top and bottom. Then fold the 19 x 2″ (47.5 x 5 cm.) strip in half lengthwise, turn under the raw edges, encase the raw edges of the apron top and bottom, baste and machine-stitch all the way across. (Fig. 14). Put aside.

Alice's, Mad Hatter's and March Hare's skirts:

The skirts for Alice, the Mad Hatter, and the March Hare are made together. With right sides facing pin the solid color cotton material to the print material at the hemline, or along the 36″ (90 cm.) edge. Leave a ¼″ (6 mm.) seam and baste it. Remove pins. Machine-stitch the sections together along the hemline. (Fig. 15). Remove basting thread.

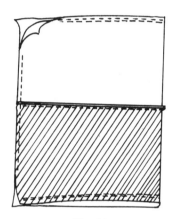

Fig. 16

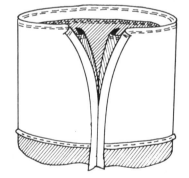

Fig. 17

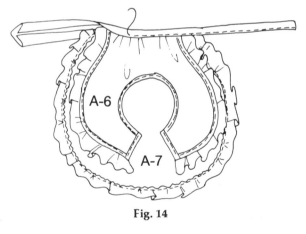

Fig. 14

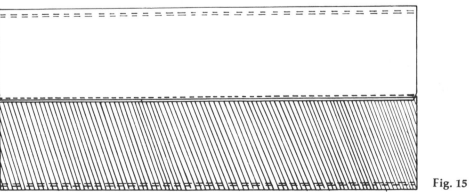

Fig. 15

Machine-stitch gathering stitches on the other two 36″ (90 cm.) edges, but don't pull to shape as yet. Fold the fabric in half with the right sides facing so that the piece now measures 23½ x 18″ (58.75 x 45 cm.) and baste along the 23½″ (58.75 cm.) edge. (The previously stitched seam now faces itself.) Measure 2″ (5 cm.) in from each end—along basted edge—and mark with pins. (Fig. 16). Next, machine-stitch between these pin marks, back-stitching at the beginning and end to secure the seam. Remove pins and basting thread.

Now turn this tubular piece inside out, wrong sides facing, and match the top raw edge as shown in illustration. (Fig. 17). Top-stitch along the hemline. The raw edges become the skirt waistlines. The seams become the center backs of the skirts.

Alice's, Mad Hatter's and March Hare's waistbands:

With right sides facing, fold the print waistband strip—10 x 1¾″ (25 x 4.5 cm.)—in half lengthwise and machine-stitch each end. Back-stitch to make them secure. Next, turn the piece to the right side and press. Pull to shape the top raw edge of the print skirt to fit the waistband. Turn under one right side raw edge of the band and pin to the right side top raw edge of the print skirt, matching each end with the center-back seam of the skirt. Baste, remove pins and machine-stitch. Remove basting thread.

Flip the waistband over the top of the skirt and, turning under the remaining raw edge of the band, hemstitch it to the other side to encase the top raw edge of the same skirt. (Fig. 18). Repeat this procedure with the other waistband to encase the top raw edge of the solid color skirt at the waist.

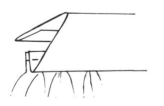

Fig. 18

Mad Hatter's hat:

Baste and machine-stitch (H-3) together as marked on pattern. Then baste and machine-stitch the top (H-5) to this cylinder on the wrong side. Then baste and machine-stitch the brim (H-4) to the other edge of the cylinder. Remove basting thread and turn hat right side out. Now stitch the edges of the band (H-6) and slip it over the cylinder. Stitch the feathers (H-7) to the band on the inside. Slip a cylindrical piece of cardboard into the hat to help keep its shape. Stitch hat to the Mad Hatter's head.

Mad Hatter's shirt:

Baste and machine-stitch the two sections of back (H-13) to the front (H-14) at the shoulders, right sides facing. Hem the armholes, then with notches matching, machine-stitch down the sides. Remove basting thread. Turn shirt right side out. Fold under along dotted line (on pattern) and hemstitch shirt to the Mad Hatter.

Mad Hatter's jacket:

Baste and machine-stitch the back (H-10) to the two sections of the front (H-9) at the shoulders. Set in the sleeves (H-11) at the armholes, baste and machine-stitch. (Fig. 19).

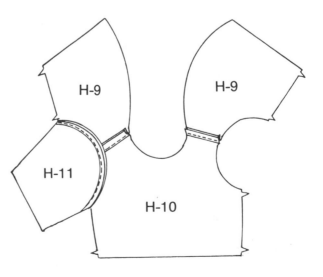

Fig. 19

Then baste and machine-stitch down the sleeves and, with notches matching, baste and machine-stitch down the sides of the jacket. Remove all basting thread. Turn jacket right side out and put on the Mad Hatter. Turn back the lapel to make the jacket appear as if it is double-breasted, and hemstitch the button (H-8) at the V of jacket.

Mad Hatter's bow tie:

With right sides facing, baste and machine-stitch the two sections of the bow tie (H-12) where indicated on the pattern, leaving a small opening for turning. Remove basting thread and turn bow tie right side out. Stitch the opening closed. Now take a small strip of felt and wrap it around the middle of the bow tie, and stitch at the back. Put aside.

March Hare's vest:

Slip the vest (M-7) on the March Hare. Stitch at the back of the shoulders and sides to secure. Now cut along the middle of the front. Place one side over the other and stitch on two buttons.

March Hare's jacket:

This jacket is made in the same way as the Mad Hatter's (see above). Put jacket on the March Hare and stitch closed only at V of jacket. (March Hare's jacket does not have a button.) Now add half a snap at V of jacket to hold the Queen of Hearts.

March Hare's bow tie:

Wrap a black felt strip around the middle of bow tie (M-6), and stitch at the back. Put aside.

Queen of Hearts:

The Queen of Hearts is made from three felt pieces. Red (Q-1) for the heart, orange for the crown (Q-2), and white for the face (Q-3).

Using the illustration (Fig. 20) as a guide, draw the features with a pencil onto the face. Embroider the features with a single strand of embroidery floss. Use red for the nose and

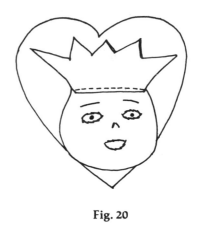

Fig. 20

mouth, working in an outline stitch. Use light blue for the eyes, again working in an outline stitch. The iris is also light blue, but worked in a French knot. Use black for the eyebrows, one straight stitch for each eyebrow.

Now hand-stitch the three pieces (Q-1, Q-2, Q-3) together as shown in illustration. (See Fig. 20). Add the other half of the snap at the back.

FINISHING

Secure the Mad Hatter and the March Hare by stitching them together at the neck with heavy-duty thread. Then stitch the pink felt bow tie to the March Hare and the cotton bow tie to the Mad Hatter to conceal the hand-stitching at the neck.

Put the solid color skirt on the Mad Hatter and the March Hare. The seam should be at the back. Hand-stitch the waistband to the dolls and hand-stitch the skirt's seam closed. Turn the doll upside down and hand-stitch the other waistband to Alice. Hand-stitch the skirt's seam closed. Put on the apron and hemstitch the apron top together behind the neck.